AF422855

AF422855

LAST FLIGHT FROM HAVANA

Last Flight from Havana: A Memoir of Cuba, Family, and Faith

Copyright © 2024, Marie Quintana

All rights reserved. No part of this publication may be reproduced, distributed, or transmitted in any form or by any means, including photocopying, recording, or other electronic or mechanical methods, without the prior written permission of the publisher, except in the case of brief quotations embodied in critical reviews and certain other noncommercial uses permitted by copyright law. For permissions and information contact: info@mariequintana.com

Published by

CUBANA WINGS
PRESS

P.O. Box 670525
Dallas, Texas 75367

First Edition

Library of Congress Control Number: 2023917829

ISBNs: 979-8-9891931-0-3 (hardcover)
979-8-9891931-2-7 (paperback)
979-8-9891931-1-0 (ebook)
979-8-9891931-4-1 (hardcover with dust jscket)

Cover and book design by Patricia Bacall
Garver, www.bacallcreative.com

Printed in United States of America on acid-free paper.

LAST FLIGHT
from
HAVANA

A Memoir of Cuba, Family, and Faith

MARIE QUINTANA

CUBANA WINGS
PRESS

Dallas, Texas

"To Whom much is given, much will be required."
~ Luke 12:48

Dedication

This book is dedicated to my two loves: my father, Juan Raul Quintana, and my son, Daniel "Danny" Cummiskey. My father was a man who exemplified all the traits that God asks of a father: he was loving, gracious, caring, courageous, optimistic, hopeful, humble, giving, hardworking, joyful, and fun. He loved life, and life loved him. He was a great dancer, and a great Cuban patriot. He never forgot the pain of being unable to return home to his beloved Cuba. His unconditional love and support for me has been the North Star in my life.

My son, Danny, was a human angel whom God called too soon. He was a true servant of God—brilliant, humble, kind, and respectful. He always had a grateful heart, despite the obstacles he faced every day. He was a gentle spirit who loved God, his family, and his friends more than anything. His personality had none of the trappings of this world—no pride, no agenda, and no selfishness; he only wanted to love others without condition or restraint. I miss him dearly every day.

Contents

Starting Over

From the moment I fled my native Cuba in 1961, I have lived a life I did not plan . . . but it has been exactly the life God intended for me to live.

Along the way, I have been on a journey of transformation as my identity has shifted, and my family and my work have changed. I've grown apart from some people and closer to others, both losing and deepening relationships. And through it all, I have become better at finding blessings in every moment of change.

I strongly believe that people get to where they're supposed to be. They may think they're not supposed to be there, but everything happens for a reason, and I am no exception. I have struggled to manage the unpredictable and unexpected. We often think our lives are going to turn out one way, and then they turn out very differently. At that point, it is incumbent on us to bravely forge ahead and create a *new* life—to learn from the pain and start over.

Fear. Shock. Uncertainty. Doubt. Those were the early themes in my young life. Time and again, I had to start over, whether in a new country, new school, new job, or new relationship. This theme of "starting over" also defined the lives of my parents, two people who were forced to leave the country they loved. They had to learn a new language, a new culture, a new profession, and new ways to cope. They had to learn how to breathe, how to let go, and how to trust in God. And, as their eldest child, I watched and learned from them as they accomplished all of these things.

But of course, as everyone does, I would have to go on my own journey to absorb these lessons completely.

I was born in Cuba, grew up in a small Cajun town in Louisiana, and moved to New Orleans for high school. I studied to be a psychologist and a social worker but then changed careers many times. I have had the privilege of assuming leadership roles across diverse domains, spanning technology, sales, marketing and communications. My journey has taken me through the corridors of Corporate America and into the realm of entrepreneurship as an advisor. Remarkably, I proudly held the distinction of being the highest-ranked Latina executive within both a Fortune 50 and Fortune 500 company, a testament to my dedication, perseverance and resilience. In one unpredictable twist, at one point I even left the country to help track down a kidnapped child and rediscovered parts of myself and my identity I didn't know I'd missed.

Likewise, my personal life was marked by seismic change. I was married for twenty-three years and had three children. While we were in the midst of a painful divorce, our son was diagnosed with mental illness. I suddenly became a single mom, parenting twins who were in high school and a son who was in and out of hospitals and facilities. I had to become a domestic and professional Holy Trinity of my own: the breadwinner, the mother, and the caregiver. And once again, I found myself having to start over and learn new ways to provide for my children.

Every day, I engaged in this process of relearning how to manage my life, family, and career. Lessons I thought I'd mastered years earlier were thrown out the window as I was forced to figure out how to better take care of myself, my children, my parents, and my employees.

Then, in 2012, my father died. He had always dreamed of going back to Cuba, but he never had the chance. We couldn't even grant him his final wish: to be buried in his own country. My father's death ripped me apart. Suddenly, all the memories of Cuba that I'd forgotten, and the life I'd left behind, came flooding back.

I realized that I had spent most of my life living in two worlds. At times, I hadn't wanted to connect the two, and at other times, I had so deeply longed for them to intertwine. After all, the world that my parents lived in was so resoundingly Cuban: the food, the memories, their constant talk of the family we left behind, and our fervent hope that we would see them again.

Shortly before my father's death, my mom and I did go back to Cuba. I expected the trip to be life-changing for her, and it was. What I never expected was how much it would change *my* life. I wish I'd known then what I know now.

Like the stories of so many Cuban exiles, my story is complicated and always unfolding. As Cubans, we have not completely come to terms with the injustice of our fate. Since it left so many families and relationships in undeserved tatters, how could we?

I have family members situated just ninety miles from Miami who struggle to live with the dignity and respect every human being deserves. Some of us have lived in the United States for more than fifty years, and today we embrace cousins who visit from Cuba with a bittersweet mixture of loving and painful memories. We ask the same gut-wrenching questions over and over: "What happened to those members of our family we lost contact with?" and "What happened to my grandfather's land?"

As Cubans, we so often find ourselves in a race against time to learn about our past and to find these memories before they are erased. We have learned to persevere through disappointments and to create new lives for ourselves, yet we still find our identities tangled up in the past. We constantly fear that our memories, once so vivid, may be forgotten.

My story is far from unique. Unfortunately, there are thousands, if not millions, of people who've had to leave their country of origin because of political unrest and instability. Many came to the United States with nothing but the clothes on their backs—and ample reserves of hope and faith in God—to start new lives. They lived with gut-wrenching losses of their homes, businesses, and families. When they were forced to relocate to a new country, they had to start over from scratch.

My return trip to Cuba with my mother opened up a world inside me that I had never known existed. When my mother looked out the window of our airplane and saw the Cuban island for the first time since 1961, her lips trembled. "*Mi Cuba*," she whispered. *My Cuba.* She hugged her hands close to her chest and said a prayer while tears rolled down her cheeks.

In life, I believe you are always free to make new choices and to start over. But it takes resilience and trust in a higher power to get you through. For me, it was my faith in God. You learn to use your faith and your inner compass to make tough choices. You learn to embrace your personal freedom and to embrace your past.

That's what this memoir is all about.

When I think about "starting over," I visualize my mom, my brother, and myself getting on the last Delta plane and leaving

Havana in 1961. My parents created a new life for themselves. And, following in their footsteps, I have created new lives for myself a dozen times since.

You have that same power. You can make choices and embrace change. You can push through heartache and loss to find a better, brighter tomorrow. It may not be the life you imagined, but here's a secret: it may be even better. That has certainly been my experience, time and again.

Marcus Buckingham, the motivational author of *Find Your Strongest Life*, says we need to identify the key, defining moments in our lives and bring power to them. Then we must use that power to gain a better understanding of ourselves. Only when we understand ourselves can we share what we have learned with others.

I want to share the lessons I have learned, and show you how every change, no matter how small, can make a positive impact. I want to show you how embracing the difficult moments in your life will empower you to recognize the opportunities that lie beyond them. I want to share my defining moments that have fueled my strengths. I want you to know that you can embrace the past, learn from it, and become a better version of yourself.

These moments have not only shaped who I am, but also serve as a constant reminder that with God's help, I can handle whatever comes my way.

And so can you.

CHAPTER 1

The Last Delta Flight from Havana: November 23, 1961

The car jostled and jolted, hitting ruts in the road as my grandfather drove my mother, my younger brother, and me to the Havana airport. His hands gripped the steering wheel so tightly that his knuckles shone through his smooth, brown skin.

"*Tranquila*," my mother said to me, over and over. *Be calm. Don't worry.*

But she was worried. I could tell.

I was just a young child, but even I knew something was terribly wrong. We were racing to the airport to flee our homeland, to start a new life in the United States. We could no longer stay in Cuba; our lives were in danger. But would we make it out in time? I had every reason to be afraid.

Two years earlier, on January 1, 1959, Fidel Castro had seized power. Our beloved country had been split into two groups: those who supported Castro's Communist regime and those who did everything in their power to dismantle the new government. Overnight, my pleasant childhood had given way to pain, fear, and confusion as my extended family began to take sides.

In the nursery school I attended, teachers taught songs about Castro and instructed us on why the new Communist government was good for the country. When I told my mother what I was learning, she immediately enrolled me in a different nursery school.

During the long, sweltering evenings, my mother and grandmother prayed the rosary on the back terrace of my grandparents' house in Jovellanos, two hours outside of Havana. They prayed in secret, afraid of what the government might do if they found out.

Things were changing. Private businesses and personal possessions were being seized. Men in military uniforms went from house to house, and when they came to our house, they confiscated our car. We were all afraid. My grandfather was the third largest rice farmer and owned cattle and crops, which meant he and my uncles were prime targets. No one knew what would happen next.

My father was a sugar chemist, and during this time he was the chief sugar chemist at the Araujo Sugar Mill in Matanzas Province. He was very proud to be one of Cuba's elite "sugarmen," who were respected globally as the best plant managers and sugar chemists in the sugar milling industry.

On April 17, 1961, my father woke to booming cannons and the threatening buzz of low-flying planes. He quickly realized that Araujo was at the center of the battle to overthrow Fidel Castro. The Cuban exiles had landed on the *Bahía de Cochinos*—the Bay of Pigs—only a few miles from where my father was working. He never forgot the terror and near-death experiences he went through that day, and in the days that followed. He knew the trajectory of his life had changed forever.

I was not old enough to read or understand, but my parents remember the newspaper headlines: "1,200 US-Sponsored Anti-Castro Exiles Invade Cuba at Bay of Pigs; Attackers All Killed or Captured by Cuban Forces."

The Bay of Pigs. Those four words have become an indelible part of the cultural memory of America. But for my family in 1961, these words did not represent abstract history. They related to real events in our lives that cloaked our days in dread and filled our nights with terror. We saw what had once been private property confiscated by the Cuban government and the lives of everyone around us were shattered as land was taken and people were executed. Chaos and worry were uninvited guests, but always in our homes.

One night when we were all asleep, we heard a knock on the door. It was about eleven o'clock at night. Trembling, my grandmother answered. Three tall men in military uniforms stood on our doorstep, casting long shadows into our house. They asked for my grandfather. When my grandfather came to the door, he was immediately handcuffed, shoved into a truck, and taken away, seemingly for being a property owner.

I was in shock as I watched the truck drive off into the night. I would never forget the look of abject horror on my grandfather's face as they dragged him away from us. My mother and grandmother screamed and wailed as the gravel crunched beneath the truck's tires. We had no idea what was going to happen to him. Would he be thrown in jail? Would he be killed? We had heard terrible stories, and we did not sleep that night. We held onto one another, crying and praying, fearing the worst.

Around dawn the next morning, a truck stopped in front of our house again and the men inside threw my grandfather out onto the street. He was disheveled and his glasses were broken, but he was home. Apparently, Castro's regime had been rounding up suspects all night, and since the prisons were full, they drove my grandfather around all night and then dumped him back at home in the morning. It could have been a lot worse.

I started hearing sirens at night. The roar of planes flying low over our house frightened me. I stopped eating. I cried constantly. The only way I could dampen the noises was to hide under my bed, where I thought no one could find me.

My mother, concerned about my health, took me to see my pediatrician. The doctor did some tests and couldn't find anything physically wrong with me. He told my mother to take me to a psychiatrist in Havana. The psychiatrist said I was going through a "situational traumatic experience." He prescribed Play-Doh!

The world raged around me as I sat at home with my Play-Doh, pressing it into colorful shapes and figures. Surprisingly, the toy was helpful. The soft dough gave me a way to occupy my mind and hands, a means of calming myself when I was on the cusp of panic. Years later, when I bought Play-Doh for my own children, I would think of it as medicine: a tool to make you feel better, even during the worst of times.

My mother worked hard to keep my mind off the disturbing news all around us. She forbade the adults in our family to talk about Castro or Cuban politics in front of me. She knew that I was like a sponge; I absorbed everything, including all the terror and uncertainty. The adults became more afraid as our situation worsened, and that frightened me even more. It was truly our faith in God that brought us together. Faith gave us the strength and hope that we would find a way through this.

But my mother couldn't shield me from everything. I heard whispers. My parents were becoming convinced the only solution was to take me and my younger brother, Raul, out of the country.

Years later, my mother explained to me that the government had ordered children aged eleven and older to be taken away to training camps, where they would absorb the government's propaganda without any parental interference. My parents feared the Communist government would exert this influence over our lives forever.

They felt a great sense of urgency to get us out of the country. My parents and I had travel visas because we had visited the United States before, when my father had worked in southeastern Louisiana during the sugar cane season. At that time, I'd made my first trip to a Louisiana sugar mill, but my brother, Raul, who was only two years old, had stayed in Cuba with my grandparents. Now we had to wait for his temporary vacation visa. It would permit him to travel to the United States and stay for up to three months during the sugar season.

After the Bay of Pigs shook us all, my father's perseverance helped him to negotiate a contract with Terrebonne Southeast Corporation Sugar Mill, and he went to Louisiana on a work visa. My mother, Raul, and I tried to be patient while he was away, but every day we anxiously awaited any news.

Meanwhile, my mother started making plans to leave. Those who didn't know us well thought we were simply traveling to the United States to be with my father while he worked during the sugar season. They thought nothing was out of the ordinary, but those in our intimate family circle knew the truth.

When my father was granted refugee status in the United States, he obtained the visa for Raul. Then he put into motion the events that would change my life forever: he completed the paperwork that would bring my mother, Raul, and me to the United States.

"*Tranquila,*" my mother said, as my grandfather's car sped over the bumpy road to the airport. She squeezed my hand. "*Tranquila,* Tere."

"Tere" was the name my father and mother called me. Teresita is my middle name in honor of Santa Teresita.

It was November 23, 1961, the day we left Cuba forever.

The day was full of weeping. As we sped along, my maternal grandfather stopped briefly at the home of my paternal grandparents so we could say good-bye. Only then did they understand the full implications of our journey. My grandmother hugged me to her chest. She smelled of flowers and spices. She cried and cried. Their loss would be fathomless, and they begged us to change our minds and stay.

But they also knew Cuba was no longer safe for us. My brother and I were young, with so much life ahead of us. The country was being crushed by the iron fist of communism. We had to get out.

A short time later, my grandfather announced: "*Aquí estamos,*" as we pulled into the Havana Airport. *We're here.* I held onto my mother with one hand and my little brother with the other. We stepped out of the car.

The airport was in utter chaos. People were panicking, children clinging to their parents and parents clinging to their children. Men and women staggered out of the airport after putting their kids on airplanes and sending them off in hopes of a better tomorrow.

This was Operation Pedro Pan, the mass exodus of Cuban children to the United States. Later, I would learn this underground operation was one of the largest recorded exoduses of unaccompanied youth in the Western Hemisphere. My heart goes out to all the Cubans who were part of Operation Pedro Pan for all of the painful decisions forced on parents and the journeys of the children who were forced to start over in a strange country without them. Some were never reunited with their families.

My mother later told me she and my father had signed Pedro Pan papers to release their parental rights and guarantee that we could travel unaccompanied just in case, at the last minute, she was unable to board the plane with Raul and me. I'm glad I didn't know that at the time. My hands were shaking as we walked through the airport terminal where the corridors were strewn with sobbing, terrified families. Raul was crying too. He had no idea what was happening, but even *he* knew our lives would never be the same.

My mother tried desperately to keep her own hands steady. She blinked back the tears. I didn't fully comprehend it then, but she was leaving her homeland, not knowing if she would return. Would she ever see her family again?

The time was coming when we would have to say one final goodbye. My grandfather knelt and clasped my brother and me to him. His body was racked with sobs as we hugged for the last time. Then he embraced my mother and told her to be strong. He cupped her chin in his hand.

My grandfather waved at us, appearing smaller and smaller as we moved into the line to board our plane. Tears were streaming down my mother's face.

Two men in dark clothes blocked our path. Their voices were gruff, but they were not wearing Castro's military uniform.

"We need to see your bags," they said.

My mother, terrified, relinquished our luggage. The men were airport officials, we realized, as they began rifling through our things. We were only allowed forty-one pounds per family, and our bags were too heavy. They took out some of our clothes and my mother's jewelry and then made her strip off the jewelry she had worn to the airport. She cried even harder as she unclasped her necklace and removed her bracelet and rings that were given to her as gifts by my father.

They continued to confiscate our belongings, piece by piece, until we passed the forty-one-pound limit. Finally, the men stepped aside and let us through. My mother's neck was beaded with sweat, and her face was wet with tears. We were the only non-Delta Airlines family to board the plane; all the other passengers were Delta employees evacuating from Cuba. Moments after we boarded, the flight crew took their seats and announced that we would be leaving for the United States.

The flight to New Orleans was only sixty minutes, but it was the most significant and painful hour of our lives. I remember it now in a haze, almost like a bad dream. I can no longer recall the scene in vivid colors. It is a blurry, black-and-white landscape of fear and loss.

My mother, on the other hand, says that she remembers every aching detail. She remembers the crying on the plane; she said there was not one person who did not have tears rolling down his or her face. She could tell you the color of the dress she was wearing and the way she had styled my hair. She could describe the scent of her father's shirt as she held him for the last time. She was leaving behind everything she had ever known.

It was the last Delta flight to leave Havana before the planes were grounded, and we had made it on board. We had escaped.

But my journey had only just begun.

CHAPTER 2

White Dress Day

A year after our arrival, I lay awake on a hot summer night, unable to sleep, listening to my father and mother speaking Spanish in hushed tones.

"I am worried," my father said, his voice low. "Until the sugar season starts, I don't know how to find paying work."

"I know," whispered my mother. "But God is watching over us. We will find a way."

"I don't speak the language. I don't know the customs. We are foreigners here."

"We will be fine."

The bayou air was humid and sticky, and my parents' words struck fear in my young heart. We had been living in a refugee housing project in New Orleans for almost a year. We were blessed to have the Catholic Charities organization to help us find housing and provide for our needs. The apartment we lived in consisted of only two small rooms; on all sides we were surrounded by other Cuban refugees trying to cope with our emergency exodus from our country. Sometimes I would wake in the middle of the night to the sound of crying coming from a neighboring apartment.

When we arrived in America, my father was still working as a sugar chemist. But since the end of the sugar season, he had struggled to find steady employment. He sold cigars, delivered pizza, and drove two hours each way to work at a wood mill, returning home every night utterly exhausted. He spoke no English, which made it nearly impossible to find a better situation.

"Tomorrow I have an interview at a sugar refinery in Reserve," he told my mother. (Reserve is a small community about forty miles from New Orleans.)

Her voice brightened. "That's wonderful!"

He smiled, maybe for the first time in months. "I hope to get the job of chief sugar chemist. I will be able to do what I love to do."

The next day, the sugar refinery offered my father a position, and within a month's time, we had moved to Reserve, where sugar was king.

My father was the first of a handful of Cuban-refugee sugar chemists who had escaped Cuba with their families and ended up in this small Cajun town. Like my father, many of these chemists had trained under Julio Lobo, the "King of Sugar" in Cuba.

To a five-year-old, Reserve was a strange and wondrous place. The town was American, but it was Cajun, too, full of distinct customs and flavors. I can still taste the distinctive spices of Cajun cuisine and remember the curiosity those flavors inspired. The Cajuns made their own sausage, called *boudin,* and they used a spicy hot sauce we had never been exposed to; it burned our lips and singed our tongues. Their famous crawfish looked to me like a cross between a lobster and a bug.

We were foreigners in a world so strange that it might as well have been another planet. In this place, no one had heard the name "Fidel Castro." Castro was all my parents and the other Cuban immigrants wanted to discuss, yet no one in Reserve cared. Most people didn't even know who he was.

But, in other ways, we weren't so different from the Cajuns. It was very important to both cultures to make sure our families were enjoying life, and cooking and eating were a huge part of that. Although our cuisines were different, the Cajuns also seemed to like beans (red, though, not black). My family began finding small areas of commonality. Later in life, I would nickname my family the "Cajun Cubans."

But even as we started sharing our unique ethnic dishes, the language difference was difficult. And it wasn't just Spanish and English; the disparity was complicated further by the French influence. Many of the town's residents were Acadians, direct descendants of the French colonists who settled in Canada and the northern US before resettling in Louisiana. They had the French names to prove it.

The people of Reserve were a close-knit group of large, extended families with surnames we could not easily pronounce like Boudreaux, Guillot, and Thibodeaux. We wondered if all Americans had names so difficult.

"*Cómo se pronuncia 'Thibodeaux,' Mama?*" I asked.

"*No lo* sé," she said. *I don't know.*

I practiced saying the word in front of the bathroom mirror, the tricky consonants getting stuck on my tongue.

The truth was, I already knew more English than my mother. My parents spoke barely a word of English. I knew a few words but had trouble with full conversations, so I was still a long way from mastering the language.

At the same time I was learning English, I was learning to speak the Cajun dialect. Some words I thought were common in English I later found out were only common in southern Louisiana. I remember using "cher" to describe a darling person or cute thing, or to end a sentence: "We gon pass a good time, yeah, cher." I pronounced "ask" as "ax" and "that" as "dat."

Later in my life, when I pronounced a word I had said a certain way in Reserve, people were quick to correct me. At first, I felt confused, then embarrassed, afraid that people thought I sounded uneducated. I eventually thought it was cool to sound Cajun. But when I was six, my tenuous grasp of the language threatened to expose me as the refugee I was. I wanted so much to be "normal." I only spoke when spoken to because I was so afraid of making a mistake and being laughed at by the other children. Kids are cruel, and I knew one careless slip would label me an outsider, unmistakably as someone who was unequivocally "other."

One day, that's exactly what happened.

It was a few days before my first class picture. Our first-grade teacher, Mrs. Landry, gave us specific instructions, and I strained to listen and understand. My parents were already leaning heavily on me to translate in this brave new world.

So I went home and told my parents what my teacher had told us.

"I have to dress in an all-white outfit," I said in Spanish.

I saw the worry etched on my mother's brow. She pressed her lips together. I did not own an all-white outfit, and we had no money to buy one.

"*¿Qué vamos a hacer?*" I asked my mother. *What are we going to do?*

I was upset. I had a strong desire to follow the rules. Mrs. Landry had specifically told us to wear all white, and if I didn't do it, I would draw attention to myself—not just as an outsider but also as someone who couldn't follow the rules. I was horrified. Like most children, I just wanted to fit in.

When my mother saw how worried I was, she squeezed my hand. "*No te preocupes,*" she said. *Don't you worry.* I could see the wheels in her brain spinning as she worked out exactly what we would do.

We couldn't afford a whole new outfit, but we *could* afford materials to make one. My mother and I went shopping for white shoes, white socks, and white fabric. We had little money, but we stretched what we had to make it work.

I paced our tiny apartment as my mother sewed a crisp, white cotton skirt for me to wear.

"*No te preocupes,*" she said again. She had sewing pins in her mouth, and the words came out muffled.

I nodded, not wanting to displease her.

I tried to be calm, and yet I was anything but. It seemed like such a simple thing to wear all white, but it wasn't simple. Not for us. Not for me. Every day at school, I was painfully aware that I didn't fit in. My thick Spanish accent, my stilted vocabulary, and the clothes I wore—most of which were hand-me-downs from my father's friends who had helped us flee Cuba—made me stand out.

I knew I was smart and I'd always been a good student, but now I was at a strange school where all lessons were taught in a foreign language. There was no way to "just blend in."

As my mother sewed, I sat on the floor, shut my eyes, and pressed my fists into my forehead. My American school was scary and foreign. Sometimes it felt like a struggle just to walk through the halls, trying to act like I belonged. I didn't want to stand out. I was worried that if I didn't wear all white, as Mrs. Landry had instructed us, I would draw undue attention to myself. Adjusting to my new life was hard enough without being labeled as the weird kid at school.

"Tere," my mother said quietly, using my nickname. "¡*Mira!* *Look!*

When I opened my eyes, I saw my mother had performed a miracle. In addition to the crisp white skirt, she had sewn me a perfect white blouse. She held it out for me, her face beaming. I was thrilled.

"It's perfect!" I cried. It was beautiful and white—exactly what the teachers wanted—and when I tried it on, I felt like a princess. I twirled around in my brand-new outfit and felt a surge of optimism. Most days, I did not fit into my strange and scary school, but I nursed a secret hope that someday, somehow, that would all change. And now I knew it with certainty.

Today would be the day!

I was photo ready, and more than that, I was ready to belong.

My father drove me to school in our rickety car. We were lucky to have a car at all; many Cuban refugees were forced to rely on rides from friends and family, which made it difficult to get to and from work, or take their children to school.

I steadied myself by holding onto the dashboard, not wanting to get dust on my outfit. I was sitting primly on a thin towel my mother had spread out on the front seat. She knew I was afraid of messing up my pretty white skirt.

I was smiling as my father pulled into the schoolyard. But all at once, the smile slid off my face. My classmates were playing rambunctiously, enjoying their last taste of freedom before the bell rang and school started. My jaw dropped as I scanned their outfits, and my heart caught in my throat as we approached the drop-off point. To my horror, my schoolmates were dressed in all the colors of the rainbow, in vibrant, dazzling jumpers, shirts, jeans, jackets, and skirts. The colors were so bright they hurt my eyes.

Desperately, I searched for any boy or girl dressed in white. The truth went off like a bomb in my head: *No one is wearing white.* I had gotten the instructions wrong. When my teacher told us what to wear, she had said to wear anything *but* white. All my fellow students had understood her, but I'd misinterpreted her words. I'd turned everything Mrs. Landry said upside down.

I felt hot tears burning down my cheeks as nausea crept into my stomach. I felt shame overtake my body as the reality of not fitting in became apparent.

"*Está bien,*" my father assured me, kissing me on the head. *It's all right.*

But I was paralyzed. I couldn't get out of the car. It felt the opposite of all right. It felt like I was wearing a huge sign on my forehead announcing, "I DO NOT FIT IN! I'M DIFFERENT!" And judging by the looks I was already getting from my schoolmates, I might as well have been wearing a real sign.

"Please," I pleaded with my father. "Please take me home. I feel sick . . . "

I was hoping I could immediately develop a serious illness, because the thought of staying there at school as the obvious black sheep—though *white* sheep would have been more accurate— was too horrible to consider. I wanted nothing more than to go home.

My father looked me in the eye and took a deep breath. "*Yo se que esto es duro pero nosotros hemos pasado cosas duras y tu puedes pasar por este día. No le pongas atención a esos muchachos. Tú eres fuerte y tu vas a tener un buen día. Te quiero mucho.*"

I know this is hard, but we have been through many hard things before. You can get through this day. Do not pay any attention to these kids. You are strong and you will have a good day. I love you very much.

My eyes misted over. I wanted so much to believe him. I grabbed my homework and stepped shakily out of the car. My dad wanted me to hold my head up high, and I did not want to disappoint him.

As my father drove away, I stood in the schoolyard, tears stinging my eyes. I was too paralyzed to wave goodbye. But my father was right. We had been through hard things before. We had left our homeland behind, our family, our whole life. The least I could do was hold my chin up on a day when I was dressed in the wrong clothes.

I felt many pairs of eyes on me as I walked stiffly inside. The fear was a solid knot in my stomach. I wished the other kids would stop looking at me. But the silent stares weren't the worst of it. As I walked down the hall, some students began to tease me. I heard the taunts thrown in my direction.

"Look at the spic!"

A group of boys pointed and laughed.

"Look at that dumb spic in white. She looks like she's going to Communion or something."

I didn't understand the word, but the tone of their voices felt like a slap in the face. I shut my eyes tightly, determined to keep the tears from flowing. I wanted to run back down the hall and out the door; I wanted to chase after my father, even though I knew his car was now a tiny speck in the distance. I wanted my papi to come back and pick me up, to take the pain away.

But I didn't do any of those things. I set my jaw. I gritted my teeth. I tried to hold my head high as I walked past those boys and all the others who said cruel things and gave me nasty looks.

I was the only Hispanic at the school, and I got called "spic" more that day than I ever had before. I was dressed in such a bizarrely "un-American" outfit. Even after school-picture day, they never let me live it down. It was as if I'd committed a transgression, some kind of sin, for being different. I was a foreigner, an outsider, an outcast.

But that day I put one foot in front of the other and kept on going. My stomach was in knots, and every time I tried to speak, a lump rose in my throat. I couldn't look at the people who were harassing me. I looked down at my feet, or gazed past them down the hall, as if I could see ahead into a tomorrow where I wouldn't be mocked or scorned.

It was a horrible day, but I survived it—and I went on to survive many more days like it. I made that White Dress Day my defining moment. It was the first day I internalized the pain of being different—the first time I knew, unequivocally, that I didn't belong. And though at the time that difference was just about the worst thing I could imagine, accepting it was actually the most courageous thing I could have done.

In *The Gifts of Imperfection*, Brené Brown talks about how important it is to tell your story. I started on this journey for the first time as an adult, when my friend Fawn Germer wrote about White Dress Day in her 2007 book, *The NEW Woman Rules: More Than 50 Trailblazers Share Their Wisdom*.

When Fawn asked my permission to use my "White Dress Day" experience in her book, I was horrified at first. The visceral memory of my embarrassment still triggered so much shame in me. But I soon realized that I was not alone: every woman has a similar story. I, and the other women whose stories appeared in the book, shared painful moments. But we were brought together by our resilience, and by our ability to claim our stories, move forward, and use them to help other women.

Today, I use this moment to fuel my purpose and inspire me to persevere and take risks. **I am different** has been transformed into **I am proud to be the unique person God intended me to be.**

We are different. We all bring uniqueness to this world, and sometimes you have to go through adversity to appreciate it.

As a little girl, I learned that no matter what the fire is ahead of you, the only thing you can do is go headfirst into it. You will get to the other side, and in order to get there, you first learn how to sit in your uncomfortable feelings.

Talking about the White Dress Day helped me heal from that painful moment, and that process has provided guidance for my life. It also helped me understand the heartache and loss my parents experienced when they left their homeland. My dad was right: we had gone through something so much harder than what I faced at school that day. My family never stopped feeling the loss, although they learned to cope with that pain in order to thrive and flourish. My father's words helped put it all in perspective: "*Tú eres fuerte*," he told me that day. *You are strong.*

Our fears are just that: fears. As Zig Ziglar once said, "FEAR has two meanings: 'Forget Everything And Run,' or 'Face Everything And Rise.'"

I have learned to use my difficult moments as a patchwork, "a life quilt" of defining moments. These moments give me confidence. They show me that God has filled my life with grace. In light of that, nothing is too hard to handle.

Tú eres fuerte. You are strong.

CHAPTER 3

Two Separate Cultures, Two Separate Worlds

"It's starting!" I called out from my spot on the living room couch. "Our show is on!"

My brother Raul came racing in to join me. Then came Juan Carlos, my youngest brother, who had been born three years after we arrived in the United States. I'd started calling him "Johnny" so he'd have an American name, unlike Raul and me, and the name had stuck: the rest of the family now called him Johnny too.

Johnny was too little to understand what was going on, but he loved watching TV. He grinned up at us as he plopped down on the couch beside me.

My mother frowned as she walked into the living room. "*No entiendo ese programa,*" she said. *I don't understand that show.*

She sat down beside us, keeping her arms folded snugly across her chest.

"*No me gusta . . .*" she began, but I shushed her. I didn't care if she liked it or not. *Leave It to Beaver* was on.

I wanted nothing more than to be like the Cleavers, like June Cleaver, or like the girls at school that Wally and Beaver had crushes on, with their neat dresses. The Hispanic population in

America at that time was around 3.5 percent. In Reserve, the percent was even more scant. I was constantly aware that I was different from 96.5 percent of the country, and I didn't like it.

I searched everywhere and still could not find a sign of anyone in my environment who looked or talked like my family or me. There were no Spanish-language TV shows, and television was our compass for how we should act and what kind of family was acceptable. I figured watching *Leave It to Beaver* was the best chance I had at understanding American culture and how to look, talk, and act like everyone else.

But my mother didn't like it. "*Vamos a ver a* Lucy," she said as she turned the dial to another channel. *We're going to watch* Lucy.

Instantly, Lucille Ball and Desi Arnaz flooded the screen.

Even though my mother didn't understand English, she loved watching *I Love Lucy*. It was the one thing we could all agree on as a family. At least in this show, we saw someone we recognized: the character of Ricky Ricardo. Television was finally showing us a successful Cuban man who had "made it" in the United States. Every now and then, he spoke a word or two of Spanish, and we all got so excited. Ricky Ricardo seemed to be accepted by mainstream Americans. My family took that as a very good sign.

And yet, *Leave It to Beaver* portrayed an ordinary American family, while *I Love Lucy* was more of a comedy. We sometimes had the uncomfortable feeling that Ricky's differences were considered inherently funny. People laughed at his difficulties in being understood, his silly accent, and his wildly gesticulating hands. He wasn't the one making the joke; more often than not, he was the butt of it.

I watched my brothers' faces as they saw Ricky Ricardo playing his bongos and being made fun of for the way he spoke English. I was tired of the stares we got whenever we went to the grocery store, or when my mom yelled at us in Spanish to get in the car. The minute we started speaking, people would stare and sometimes whisper to one another.

"I like the Cleavers," I grumbled in English. "Why can't our family be more like them?"

"*Qué?*" my mother asked.

"Nothing," I said. I knew she couldn't understand me. "Never mind."

"*Dijo que no le gusta nuestra familia,*" Raul said in Spanish. *She said she doesn't like our family.* I glared at him. This wasn't what I had said, even if it was exactly what I had meant.

Of course I loved my family. I felt comfortable while I was in their protected nest. But it was hard. I was ten years old, and everyone I knew at school was American. No one was from Cuba.

Ever since I'd learned English, I had started looking everywhere I could for clues about how to be more "American." I watched *The King Sisters, The Ed Sullivan Show*, and Elvis Presley movies. No one in these movies ever ate Cuban food. I liked Cuban food, but I wanted my parents to cook American food too: hamburgers and hotdogs with ketchup, and meatloaf and casserole and roast chicken and cookies and pie, just like the people on TV.

I also wanted my mom to make Cajun food, like gumbo or crawfish, like the people who lived around us. Every meal we ate was Cuban food. We would drive to New Orleans once a month to shop at a Latin market, and we'd go to Schwegmann's, where my mother would buy Cuban black beans and spices. We never veered away from the Cuban staples of black beans and rice, pork, *arroz con pollo*, and *picadillo*. And to this day, those dishes remain my all-time favorites, even if I was desperate for anything else back then.

Around this time, I began to realize that I lived in two separate worlds. I came to think of the world of my parents, who did not speak English and did not understand American culture, as the "Old World." Their world was all about Cuba, and it was the only life they knew. They constantly had Spanish-language radio on, listening for any news that might signal the possibility of returning to their country. Communication with Cuba was sparse; every month or so, we might get a letter. In the early years, many of my parents' letters back home were intercepted once they arrived in Cuba, and few of the letters from our family in Cuba ever made it all the way to us.

My father, the youngest of thirteen brothers and sisters, grieved for his family. His beloved brothers had started the "Bar Hermanos Quintana," with several locations in Havana. It was frequented by many famous musicians, including Benny Moré, one of the greatest Cuban singers of all time. The family lost all of their businesses and my dad was never reunited with parents.

But, now and then, some of the letters made it through to us. My father received a birthday letter from his parents in 1962, and the message from his parents was both touching and heartbreaking:

My beloved and dear son, I write you this letter to remember you and wish you a very Happy Birthday. I know you will be celebrating with your wife and children. May God grant all of you good health and good fortune.

We are eager to hear from you. Here everyone is fine. I know Antinea will have to struggle a lot because now she is alone doing everything. We are having hot days that are hard to bear, it has not rained enough.

Let's see how the year ends. Love and kisses to Antinea and the children and receive a warm hug from your parents. Please do not forget us.

Mela and Loreto

The TV news was a major source of information for most people, but my parents couldn't understand what was being said. To make matters worse, the American news never mentioned Cuba. It was as though my parents' homeland did not exist.

And when it was mentioned, the reality between our experience and the TV was impossible to reconcile. Just as easily as he'd introduced the Jackson Five and the Muppets to America, Ed Sullivan gave a fawning interview back in 1959 with Fidel Castro. He described Castro as a "fine young man, and a very smart young man" and told his viewers that "with the help of God and our prayers, and with the help of the American government, the [Cuban George Washington] will come up with the sort of democracy down there that America should have." My family had suffered a tremendous loss; how could we share those same feelings?

Even as a young girl, I knew instinctively that we would have to learn about our new culture very quickly if we wanted to survive. Yet my parents insisted on spending their time sitting around, longing for news from our family in Cuba. They had a bag packed in case they heard on the news that Castro had died, and they kept that bag packed for ten years.

They couldn't give up hope. My parents constantly talked and prayed about going back home. We moved to four different houses in Reserve, always renting instead of buying because my parents didn't want to own a house. They refused to put down roots in America. They believed that, any day now, we'd be going home.

But, at ten years old, I had spent more than half of my life in America. America *was* my home. This was the New World, the second world I inhabited. I couldn't afford not to live in it.

Every day, I tried to translate the southern-Louisiana Cajun culture into a Cuban culture that my parents could understand. This was a huge part of my experience growing up. The White Dress Day in first grade was not an isolated incident. I went through many experiences like that, and soon I began to take on a leadership role in my family. When I didn't know what to do, I would make a cup of tea with loose tea leaves, and then swirl the dregs around in the cup, searching for patterns that might give me a clue.

I had learned a lot from American TV. I had started to make friends. I loved to jump rope and look for four-leaf clovers, and to bring pennies to the penny parties, where sweets cost just a penny, and where I couldn't wait to eat fudge. My mother never made fudge. She made *arroz con leche*, a Cuban rice pudding. Yes, it was delicious, but I really wanted to try more American desserts.

My friend Jill had lots of desserts at her house: homemade cookies and cakes and pies. Jill knew how to sing and play the piano, and I remember the lyrics to one song in particular: "My daddy is president. What does your daddy do? I live in a big, white house on Pennsylvania Avenue." Jill didn't really live in the White House, but every time she sang that song, I couldn't help but think how different Jill's world was from mine.

At least I was finally making friends. I'd grown quite fond of Reserve, because when I could pretend not to be Cuban, I actually fit in.

My parents had different ideas. They continued to feel lonely and different. They yearned to live closer to other people who spoke Spanish. They also wanted their kids to have more opportunities, which meant living in a larger city. Most important, they wanted me to follow in my mother's footsteps and attend a Catholic, all-girls high school. Little did I know that this plan was actually in the works. One day, I found out.

"*Tenemos algo que queremos decirte,*" my mother said. *We have something we want to discuss with you.*

"We've been in Reserve for seven years," my father began. He nodded toward me. "Tere is twelve years old."

My mother turned to me. "Next year, you'll be in high school, Teresita. I think it's best for you to attend Catholic school."

I was getting nervous.

"But I'm already *in* Catholic school," I replied. I was in the middle of eighth grade, and for the last two years, I'd been attending a coed Catholic school in Reserve.

"We want to enroll you in an all-girls high school," my father said.

I started to panic.

"But there's not an all-girls Catholic high school here in Reserve."

My mother nodded.

"That's why we're moving the family to New Orleans."

"What? No! My friends are here! You can't take me away from them." *What about my life here?* "I want to graduate from a school in Reserve!"

"Your mother and I have decided this is what's best for the whole family," my father explained gently. "Teresita, you will make friends wherever you go."

I didn't want to hear anything they had to say. I was so mad at my mom. How could she do this to me? Like any twelve-year-old, I couldn't believe my parents had "ruined my life." At the time, I couldn't comprehend that the decision was about much more than just me. My parents had decided their children would have more opportunities in a larger city than in a small town. They wanted to give us the very best education they could afford, and it was obvious they would find this in a big city.

My mother did want me to follow her footsteps by attending a Catholic, all-girls high school, but she had good reason. She knew a lot about small, rural towns. Having grown up in the small town of Jovellanos, she knew the path many girls followed: they would marry, settle down, and have children. Many would never leave their small town, which meant they would not have as many opportunities in life.

"What about my friends?" I cried.

I said it in English, but she must have understood, because she answered, "*Estamos juntos y eso es lo que es más importante.*" *We have each other and that is the most important part.*

This is what they always said when something was being taken from me. I couldn't hear the truth in her words. I was too angry. Furious, I stormed out of the room.

Nevertheless, my parents pulled me out of school, moved our family to New Orleans, and enrolled me in a coed Catholic school to finish out eighth grade. I'd start at the all-girls Catholic high school that fall. I wasn't looking forward to it.

I never would have guessed how much I would end up loving New Orleans and my high school, or how much I'd adore our family's new house on Bayou St. John. My parents had been right all along: New Orleans was a wonderful place for me to be a teenager.

But of course, I didn't know that when we first arrived. I was furious at my mother for what I interpreted as her desire to make me follow the same path she had taken in Cuba. And I continued to be heartbroken that my parents and I were living in two separate cultures—and two separate worlds.

It's always difficult being a teenager, but being a teenager as an immigrant in the 1970s was even harder. I felt a sense of responsibility to my family, and having to navigate a new path without any direction was confusing. I had to build the bridge between my parents and an outside world that did not understand Cuban culture.

Of course, as a teenager, this is the last thing you want to do. You'd rather be out with your friends, dating and gossiping and going to the movies. You see the cool and sophisticated families on TV and wish your family could be more like them. My parents were not ready to accept American culture.

I soon realized that I was not the only one who has felt this way. I've often had fellow Latino immigrants come up to me after a speaking engagement and say, "You described my experience perfectly. I went through exactly the same thing. I was always looking for cues on how to fit in, watching TV shows or reading magazines. And my parents just didn't understand."

Even in the big city, my family still felt the pain of separation from their country of origin, even as they tried to adjust to their new home. Again, my family had different customs, different foods, and a different language than the people around us. We lived in an isolated community, with very few Hispanic families. I still could not relate to my culture.

These were my formative years, when I was an awkward adolescent trying to fit in. I know now that every choice my parents made for our family was based in faith. I know I have benefited from their devotion to prayer. I've watched how humbly they asked for God's guidance on every decision they had to make, and even if I wasn't always aware of it at the time, I learned much from them.

I believe that growing up in two worlds has helped me to accept ambiguity in my life. It has made me more open to taking risks in my life, both personally and professionally. I know that when I fall, I can always pick myself up and try again because I learned early in life how to start over. Starting over might mean you have to reinvent yourself. But as I grew, I realized this is nothing to be afraid of.

Quite the contrary, it can mean you are becoming the person you were always meant to be.

CHAPTER 4

Reuniting and Letting Go

"Mama!" Raul cried. "Where are they? Do you see them?" The five of us—my parents, my two younger brothers, and I—stood in the terminal of the New Orleans airport, scanning the passengers as they deplaned. My mother gripped her rosary, tears filling her eyes. She had not seen her parents in seven long years. Now they were coming here, moving to America.

"Where are they?" Raul shouted, giving voice to the anxiety we all felt. ¿Dónde están?

More and more Cubans filed off the plane. Conditions were worsening in Cuba, and Castro ruled the country with an iron fist. Flights from Cuba had resumed, and we were told that the elderly had an easier time leaving Cuba because Castro had decided that he did not need them. Now more of them were leaving every day; thousands of elderly refugees were fleeing their country to start new lives in the United States.

On this flight were two very special passengers: my mother's parents, Abuelo Carlos and Abuela Eloisa, had departed Cuba that morning. My mother had coordinated their trip so that they would arrive in New Orleans shortly after we did. They were coming to live with us.

"I see them!" Raul cried. "Abuela Eloisa! Abuelo Carlos!"

29

My brother charged toward our grandparents. He'd only been three-and-a-half years old when he'd last seen them, but he still remembered the shapes of their faces—maybe because my mother kept their pictures on the dresser in the bedroom, or maybe because the anguish and terror of our last day in Cuba had forever imprinted their faces in his memory.

And there they were—my grandparents. They looked older and smaller, and yet somehow exactly the same. My grandmother wore a neat, flowered dress, her graying hair pinned up in a bun above her neck. My grandfather wore slacks and a striped shirt, his tufts of white hair sprouting up over his ears.

"Papa," my mother gasped, the breath catching in her throat as her father approached, his gait slower than it had been when we'd seen him last. His eyes were brimming with tears.

"Papa," she sighed as he enfolded her in a hug.

Abuela Eloisa was already sobbing as she joined in the family embrace, stroking my mother's hair and neck and cheeks as if she had recovered her most precious possession in the world.

"*¡Mira,* Tere!" My grandmother dabbed her cheeks with a handkerchief and spun around to look at me. "What a beautiful young girl you are becoming!"

My grandfather grasped my hands and tried to lift me, but then he winced as he set me back down.

"It's his back," my grandmother said with a wry grin. "He's not as young as he thinks he is." She'd always had a terrific sense of humor.

They hugged Raul, who was now eleven—so much bigger than the three-year-old they'd put on that plane out of Havana. They hugged my father. And they marveled at my littlest brother, Juan Carlos, "Johnny," whom they were meeting for the first time.

"He's so American," my grandfather whispered to my mother. Despite Juan Carlos's very Cuban features, they felt the fact that he'd been born on US soil made him different. In a way, it did.

"We thought we'd never see you again," my grandmother cried, sobbing into my mother's neck. She kept laughing and crying and laughing again.

"*Estamos juntos*," my mother said, which were fast becoming her favorite words. "*Eso es lo que es más importante.*" *We are together. That's the most important thing.*

Tears flowed freely all around.

After nearly a decade, my grandparents were finally able to leave Cuba. They'd had to leave everything behind, just as we had, but they were safe in America, beyond Castro's reach.

But we were not so lonely now. In the early years, we had felt orphaned in the United States. Now we had family. A few months earlier, my mother's brother had been able to leave Cuba with his family and move to New Orleans, and now she was joyously reunited with her parents. I hadn't seen her look so happy in years. Later on, she would be reunited with her second brother. It was a blessing for her to have her whole family around her again.

My father watched the scene unfold with both joy and longing heavy in his eyes. His own parents were still in Cuba, unable to get out. He didn't know it at the time, but he would never see them again. His eleven brothers and sisters were split: six of them had stayed in Cuba, and the other six, including my father, had made it to the United States. I saw in my father the agony of a close family split down the middle, wishing every day that they could be reunited.

But in that moment, we were thrilled to have at least half of our family intact. We ushered my grandparents out of the airport, eager to take them to their new house.

The only problem was, we didn't actually *have* a house. My parents had steadfastly refused to buy a house, still hopeful they'd be able to return to Cuba someday, even as news from their homeland grew worse. But we had to live somewhere, and now that my grandparents were here, we were a family of seven. It was time to find a house of our own.

At first, we moved to a little housing project, where we lived briefly until I finished eighth grade. I hated the projects.

Then, when I was in ninth grade, we moved to a beautiful white duplex in Bayou St. John. I loved it! I had my own bedroom, the biggest in the whole house, right off the living room. And the house was a short walk across the bridge from Cabrini High, my new school. My friends would be able to come home with me after classes.

"Everything is going to be all right now," my mother said on the day my grandparents moved in. "*Estamos juntos.*" *We are together.*

But "together" wasn't always something I enjoyed. It had been seven years since I had been with so much family. I was thirteen, already unhappy about leaving Reserve to move to New Orleans—and now I had an even harder time brokering my two worlds.

I was living with my grandparents. No other teenagers I knew had this many adults to contend with! Suddenly, when I shuffled into the kitchen in the mornings for breakfast, my grandmother would be there, drinking her Cuban coffee and chiding me on the length of my skirt or the wrinkles in my shirt.

"Do you go out of the house like that?" she would cry, throwing her hands up in the air. "Your hair's a mess!"

With two more bodies in the house, the rooms always seemed crowded. I did not get to watch *Leave It to Beaver* as often anymore because my grandparents couldn't understand it. Now it seemed like all we watched was the news—with even more urgent interest in news of Cuba. I wanted to scream, "There is no Cuban news! Nobody cares about that stuff here!" But of course, I didn't want to hurt their feelings. Ever the good daughter and granddaughter, I bit my tongue.

I'd thought my parents lived in the "Old World," but that was nothing compared to the feelings of my grandparents, who might as well have been living in a different universe. My grandparents were still coping with grief at having to leave their country. They talked constantly about our hundreds of relatives who had stayed behind. My grandfather spent all day typing letters and mailing them. He would sit on the front porch every day, waiting for the mailman to bring news about the family who remained in their lost homeland.

Most days, the mailman disappointed him, because letters from Cuba took a long time to reach us, and mail service between the two countries was unpredictable. When letters did arrive, we came together as a family to hear the news. The reading of the letters always ended with my grandparents and my mother weeping.

I didn't cry. I did not remember most of the people they talked about. Our extended family was so large that I had trouble tracking the stories. The saddest times were when we got a letter saying someone had died. I would see the grief in my parents' and grandparents' eyes, but I didn't understand it. It hurt me to see them so sad, but I couldn't understand the depth of their emotion, and that frustrated me.

Sometimes I would stumble into the dining room and find my grandmother looking out the window, her eyes vacant.

"Teresita," she would murmur, beckoning to me. "Did I ever tell you the story about how your grandfather bought a store for his sister to run?" And I would stand there, itching to be out with my friends, while she recounted some long story from her faraway world.

My grandmother was a smart, caring, and determined woman. She had a wonderful sense of humor and was devoted to my grandfather. She would eventually outlive him, passing away just a few months shy of her ninety-ninth birthday. But at the time, I was young, and I didn't always have the patience to listen to her stories.

In the last months of her life, she would recite a beautiful poem: "*Nada se borra; nada se acaba.*" *Nothing is erased; nothing ever ends.*

I knew that my grandmother believed this, but sometimes I *wanted* to erase our troubled Cuban past. I wanted it to end, so that our new life could begin.

This poem came to mind recently as I talked with my aunt who was visiting from Cuba. She searched her frail memory for the names of family members who had passed, reporting on how they'd lived their last years or recalling how my grandfather's land was divided in the years after they left Cuba. She mentioned that the Cuban government wanted nothing more than to have those memories erased.

"*Nada se borra,*" I said, my grandmother's poem coming back to me. "*Nada se acaba.*" And my aunt nodded with tears in her eyes.

That poem inspired me to connect to my past. I decided to start putting the story together, the story that my kids will tell their kids someday. Telling these stories will preserve some sense of our heritage.

During those years, my new life was just beginning. I didn't have the capacity to understand how my Cuban culture was affecting me. I was living in the present. I quickly realized I would be starting at a new school with other girls who also didn't know anyone. As freshmen, we were all new and nervous, which put us on equal footing. I also noticed that, unlike my school in Reserve, Cabrini High School had a few other Hispanic students. Cabrini High, guided by the spiritual wisdom of Mother Cabrini, played a pivotal role in shaping not only my education but also in grounding my spiritual life.

After the first day of school, a few of the other girls swarmed around me. "Where are you from?" they asked. "Why do you speak Spanish?" They seemed genuinely curious, not at all judgmental or mean.

I ended up making many friends in high school, though I was the only Hispanic girl among them. I was fondly called "Kouba" within my close-knit circle. These girls fell in love with my family. They loved Cuban food and found it interesting that my grandparents lived with us.

I'd spent so many years feeling ashamed of being different, but now I had friends who *loved* that we were different. None of the girls spoke Spanish, but they seemed to enjoy hearing my brothers and my parents speak it. After a while, I even liked being called "Kouba." My new name seemed to be their way of accepting me and my family, strange as we were.

Bit by bit, my parents and grandparents began building a community of Cuban refugees in New Orleans. My grandfather had a big dominoes table on the porch, and every Sunday all the local Cuban men would come over to play dominoes and drink Cuban *cafecito*. They would still talk about Cuba—that seemed to be all anyone in my family wanted to do—but at least my parents and grandparents had found a group of friends.

I'd usually skip the dominoes games, preferring to spend all my time with Tessie, my best friend. I met Tessie at the beginning of my freshman year, and we hit it off right away. We learned we had much in common, including the same taste in clothes and music. We were both helpless at most sports, but we loved singing. I was an alto and she was a soprano. "Which is perfect," she told me, "because it means we harmonize."

And that's what we did. We complemented each other, like sisters. I'd never had a friend like her, someone who understood me so well and cared about me so much. She met my family and immediately connected to my parents, my brothers, and my grandparents. It was the same for me with her family. Tessie's parents became like second parents to me.

And if I thought my house was crowded with relatives, it was nothing compared to Tessie's house: she had nine brothers and sisters, and relatives all over the Irish Channel neighborhood of New Orleans. She told me stories about the adversity and hard times her family had endured when they first came to the United States. Her stories sounded similar to my own experience of coming from Cuba. Except for the fact that she was Irish and I was Cuban, Tessie and I could have been sisters. That's how we acted, and that's how her family treated me.

"I've never known a Hispanic person before," she told me. She wanted to know everything about my culture—our foods, our clothes, our music. Tessie was proud of her Irish heritage, and it was hard for her to understand that I didn't feel the same kind of pride. She would sometimes ask, "What's it like in Cuba?"

"I don't want to talk about Cuba!" I'd reply. It was all my parents ever talked about. I wanted to talk about America.

I taught her a few phrases in Spanish, and she got so she could speak a little to my parents and grandparents. She loved coming to our house for dinner, and trying the *arroz con pollo*, the *ropa vieja*, and the fried plantains. She was curious about everything. "*¿Puedo tomar un mojito?*" she asked innocently one night at our dinner table. *May I drink a mojito?*

My parents looked at each other uncomfortably. They did not want to offend my friend, and they loved how curious Tessie was about Cuba—but they didn't want to be responsible for providing her first rum drink either.

Then she gave them her mischievous smile, and I explained, "*Es una broma.*" *It's a joke.*

Another day, I was showing Tessie some of the clothes my grandmother had brought from Cuba—beautiful, hand-sewn dresses with rich reds and blues and bright yellows. I can't remember which one of us had the idea first; the way our brains worked, we usually had the same thought at once. Within the hour, we had Tessie wearing one of the dresses and a wig, along with a hat with a veil, and I was on the phone inviting some other friends over to the house, to meet "my aunt from Cuba." Tessie roamed around the house in that costume for hours, playing dominoes with our friends and pretending she didn't speak a word of English, before she finally took off her veil and wig and shocked everyone.

When our senior year arrived, it was time for us to start thinking about our future: What were we going to do after high school? Tessie's heart was set on going to Louisiana State University in Baton Rouge, and she wanted me to go with her. "We'll be roommates, of course!" she told me excitedly.

But I wasn't so sure. It wasn't that I didn't want to go to LSU; I absolutely wanted to go. To be honest, it was hard for me to imagine attending a college in New Orleans without Tessie. But my family could not afford to send me away to school.

My parents came up with a plan for me to go to the University of New Orleans while living at home. This made total sense to them; it meant I could get an affordable education without spending money on room and board. It never crossed their minds that I would want to go away to school, but that was exactly what I wanted. Leaving home felt like an important step to me—an important way to start my adult life—but I also understood it was not part of the Cuban culture. My parents did not want me to live away from home.

"I'm going to LSU," I announced, "or I'm not going to college."

I didn't want my decision to cost them any money, I told them. My plan was to save money from a summer job and then get another job in Baton Rouge so I could keep working while I attended school.

"I'll pay for everything," I told them.

I submitted my application to LSU, and in the spring, I was accepted. I immediately started looking for work.

When my parents saw how determined I was, they understood that this decision was important to me. I know it was hard for them to let me go to school an hour away—it would be a painful separation for them—but they soon supported my decision. My dad even helped me line up a summer job, as well as a job I could work once I got to LSU, so I could pay my tuition.

That fall, I left home to start my next adventure. It was a great experience to go away to school and begin my studies to become a psychologist. I was the only Hispanic person in my dorm. Once again, my new friends were curious about how we were able to maintain our Cuban culture.

❧

For years, it felt as though I were being pulled apart like a wishbone. When my grandparents came to live with us in New Orleans, I couldn't imagine how all of us were going to coexist under a single roof. It seemed impossible to blend cultures, young and old, Cuban and American.

I no longer wanted to keep one foot in Cuba. I was tired of always having to repeat the same stories about being Cuban to every person I met, especially when I'd go out on dates. *Where is my family from? Do they speak English? Why am I living here?*

Every now and then, I would date someone who came from a family that was not accepting of Hispanics. I can still remember one date when I was a senior in high school: he took me to his house to pick up something he'd forgotten and told me to sit low in the car because his father did not like Cubans.

Luckily, most of my friends were not like that. Thanks to the love and support shown to me by many friends, especially Tessie, I was beginning to feel more and more assimilated. What I didn't realize was how much of my culture I was leaving out of my life. I had no idea how much these decisions—which I made during a time when I thought I needed to be "assimilated"—would cost me in later years. I couldn't see the long-term effects of the many times I had to separate my two worlds because I could not bring the two together and still "fit in" or be accepted.

After I started my first year of college, my parents bought their first house. I think the purchase was a signal that they had crossed a crucial emotional line. At last, they had sadly admitted they would not be returning to Cuba, although they would hold out a glimmer of hope forever.

I could say that they started to come around to my side, but the real truth is that I have started coming around to theirs too. Only now am I beginning to realize why they yearned so deeply for their lost dreams. Now I understand what it really means to be a Cuban living your life in the United States and returning home to find your heart.

Here is the poem that my grandmother, Eloisa Estevez Rubayo, recited over and over again. We think she authored it.

Sobre la arena puse tu nombre
Con quien sonaba
Pero a medida que lo escribía
Venían las olas y me lo borraban.

Sobre la piedra lo puse luego
Por si la piedra lo conservara
Como es la roca, como es la piedra.
Nada se borra; nada se acaba.

Translated, it reads:

On the sand I wrote your name
of you I dreamed
But halfway through writing it
the waves came and erased it.

On the rocks, I wrote it later
for the rock retained it, like the rock, like the stone.
Nothing is erased; nothing ever ends.

While we are in the midst of living our lives, we are creating memories. These memories can either paralyze us or bring us understanding, forgiveness, and even joy. We can choose to write our story and to see the blessings behind every event that touches us—but that choice is up to us.

In the end, it is really about becoming the person God intended you to be. It all comes down to connecting to your authentic self. You may need to "hit the reset button," if that's a part of your path.

God wants us to be free. It is not only about immigrants or ethnicity; this is about people in general not feeling free to be themselves. It might be an illness, an addiction, or a past experience that keeps you from freeing yourself. Though my experience is different, I respect the pain you are experiencing. I've worked so hard to bring my two disparate lives together. I can relate to people who struggle to be their authentic selves in a world that can seem hostile and unforgiving. Before you judge someone, step into their shoes and walk the path they are walking.

I know I could not do the things I do today if I had not pushed myself. I had to keep working on myself and not give up. Find and use your gifts. This is the most important purpose of your life.

The best version of you is about to take the world by surprise.

Photo Album

A cherished memory: My mother proudly graduating from Immaculate Conception High School in Havana, marking the beginning of her journey into adulthood.

*Mom and Dad, newly engaged and joyfully celebrating
their commitment on my grandfather's farm.*

*Capturing a glimpse of my parents' romantic journey during
the time they lived in Cuba.*

*My first formal baby picture, marking the arrival of the first born
and first grandchild to a heartwarming and caring family.*

*As a little one, I got an early start on horseback riding, here I am
with my aunt and cousin on my grandfather's farm.*

Growing up with my younger brother for a short time in Cuba, our early childhood was filled with a sense or ordinary bliss.

At the tender age of three, sharing a moment with my dad and his co-worker on a boat called Havana.

Family bliss at Varadero Beach, alongside my brother Raul, mom and dad. A cherished and sometimes forgotten memory of the house on this stunning beach, a wedding gift from my grandfather to my mom.

Enjoying a tranquil moment with my mom and brother on my grandfather's lush farm.

THE SOUTH COAST CORPORATION

HOUMA
LOUISIANA

PRODUCERS OF
White Gold
PURE CANE
SUGAR

July 22, 1961

Sr. Juan Raul Quintana
3 RA. Esq. A Luz Caballero
Jovellanos, Matanzas
Cuba

Dear Sr. Raul:

We are attaching hereto copies of your contract for work as a Bench Chemist at our Terrebonne Factory for the coming grinding season. We would appreciate your returning them promptly so that we can make the necessary arrangements to have you enter the United States prior to the crop.

Yours very truly,

Roland L. Toups
Vice President

nlk

Enc.

This letter, offering my father a job opportunity in the United States, marked the beginning of our journey to leave our homeland.

Our initial picture, taken months after arriving in the United States, during a very challenging period we found refuge in a refugee project.

I carried this doll all the way from Cuba on the plane. Though she may appear well-worn, the bond between us was deep and enduring.

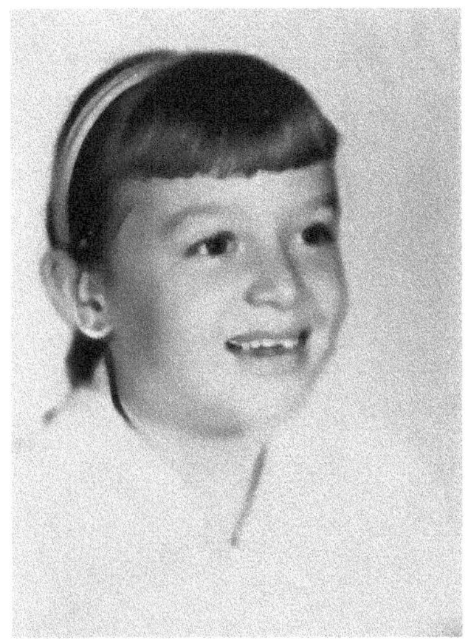

The day of my white dress picture day, a memory etched in my heart forever.

My father's reunion with two of his brothers, with one of them granted the rare opportunity to visit the United States. I vividly recall my shock when he shared that the government had denied him the simple pleasure of drinking milk for most of his adult life, forcing him to rely on sunshine for his calcium.

My maternal grandparents resided with us in New Orleans, carrying with them the enduring grief of leaving Cuba continued until their final days. Their unwavering love for each other was a cherished blessing.

PEREGRINO DE LA CARIDAD

Celebración de la Santa Misa
Plaza Antonio Maceo
Santiago de Cuba
Lunes 26 de marzo de 2012, 5:30 p.m.

Our journey back to Cuba took the form of a spiritual pilgrimage,
led by Pope Benedict XVI.

During our visit to our Cuban home, my mom and I found solace in sitting in the back patio, reminiscent of the moments she spent in this home. Amidst a profound sense of loss and sadness, we sought connection to cherished memories.

During our visit my mom was joyfully reunited with many family members, including her closest cousin, whom she regarded as a sister. Sadly, shortly after our trip her beloved cousin passed away, reminding us that time is precious.

My mom, dad and brothers coming together in celebration of a family occasion. A cherished moment in time.

Life is Meant for Dancing! My dad was the happiest when he was on the dance floor. He never needed much of a reason to throw a party, and I loved every moment of joining him in the celebration.

My mom, dad, Raul, and me, all together on our 50th anniversary of our arrival from Cuba, commemorating a significant milestone in our family's journey.

A memorable Saturday united my Cuban family and friends in Florida to celebrate my wedding, marking a beautiful moment in time. Just two days later, the unexpected loss of my beloved son Danny cast a shadow over our happiness. Amidst the heartbreak, the following Saturday saw my friends and family gathering in Dallas to commemorate Danny at his memorial service. This poignant transition from seven days of immense joy to profound sorrow was a stark reminder of life's unpredictable twists.

Mom and Dad, what an incredible legacy they have lived and have left us. What an honor to celebrate them through the narratives within these pages.

CHAPTER 5

Choices Are Never Easy: Starting a Career and a Family

My family is the center of my universe. In my Cuban culture, living close to family is a very high priority. My mother lived with her parents when she got married, and then her parents lived with her after they came to the United States from Cuba.

Raising my own family in a different city from my parents was difficult for all of us. It was hard for me to break the tradition of living close to my extended family, but it was my choice, and part of my new American identity.

My ex-husband and I met at Tulane University, where I was attending graduate school. When we first started dating, it seemed we had a lot in common, though we came from two very different backgrounds. He had a small nuclear family of Irish and German descent. It was hard for me to understand why he never visited his cousins; he only had two! There were many differences to overcome, but they did not stand in the way of our relationship at that time.

Two years later, I received my master's degree in social work, and we got married. I worked for a couple of years in New Orleans, counseling immigrants in a mental health clinic as the director of

Spanish services. But then, he was offered a job in Dallas, and my life took a big turn. Suddenly, I was faced with a life-changing decision: Could I move that far away from my parents?

While we were packing up our lives in Louisiana, my ex-husband's aunt called to tell me a major tech company in Dallas was hiring.

"They have openings, Marie," she said. "I think you should interview once you get to Dallas."

I was flattered but confused. "I don't have a degree in technology," I said.

"They're interviewing people who have master's degrees in liberal arts! The company wanted to hire people with different backgrounds and train them in everything they need to know about technology."

I was intrigued by the opportunity. I was ready for a challenge—and an opportunity to do something different from social work. I looked forward to a career that had more to do with business. I was also excited to use the skills I'd learned in social work in a business capacity.

So I researched the company, and I liked what I saw. I picked up the phone and set up an interview. They said they were eager to meet me.

On my first night in Dallas, I stared into the bathroom mirror of our new apartment and practiced answering dozens of interview questions, over and over, until I felt 100 percent prepared. The next morning, I put on a starched white blouse, tied a bow around the collar, a blue blazer and set out for the interview that would change the course of my life.

I remember it like it was yesterday. The company's regional headquarters were housed in a tall, formidable gray building. I walked into the foyer and took a deep breath. This was real, and I was ready.

A few minutes later, I strode into the office of the vice president of human resources and shook his hand. The interview began. Every single question he asked was one I'd practiced the night before.

They offered me a job the next day.

The company gave me a choice to complete an eighteen-month training program either in sales and marketing or in systems engineering. These rigorous training programs were similar to graduate business school programs and completing one program was similar to receiving an MBA.

Sales and marketing seemed to be the obvious choice. I'd come from a background in social work, and I knew how to work with people. I had good communication skills, and I believed I would excel at developing relationships with customers. There was no doubt I'd enjoy sales and marketing, and I was pretty sure I would be good at it.

I chose systems engineering instead.

Sometimes, I still don't know why I did it. I knew engineering would be the harder of the two, but I think that's *why* I did it: sales and marketing would have felt like an easy way out. If I chose to learn systems engineering, I'd know the product at the core of the company. I assumed I would eventually shift into sales and marketing, but if I had some background in engineering first, then I'd know exactly what I was selling.

The program was grueling. Learning assembler programming was not something I liked, although I knew I wanted to push myself into areas where I was not inherently comfortable. I was surrounded by people who were engineers by trade—left-brain thinkers who innately understood both the language and the field. I wasn't inclined toward engineering at all; this was a hard learning curve for me.

But I learned so many things. I learned the importance of working in teams and surrounding myself with people whose skills and strengths complemented mine. I learned the power of focus and dedication. I carried binders of books everywhere I went. My friends said I was obsessed. When they called to ask me out to dinner on the weekends, I'd tell them, "No, I can't do anything; I have to study." I have one friend who still talks about how nerdy I was during that year and a half.

But I did it, and I excelled. I became a successful systems engineer! This was the beginning of my corporate career. I'd always chosen the hardest paths, the ones that were ambitious and took everything out of me. I didn't want to simply figure things out; I wanted to challenge myself and persevere to succeed.

My career has been a diverse journey, spanning a wide range of fields and industries. I started as a systems engineer, but gradually shifted gears into technology operations, sales, marketing and communications and eventually climbing the corporate ladder to reach the positions of Vice President of Technology, Senior Vice President of Sales and Marketing and later, Executive Vice President of Communications and Chief Marketing Officer. I found myself in some unexpected places, using skills I didn't know I had — skills I had been building along the way.

When I started at the tech company, I was only twenty-four. I knew that one day I was going to have kids, but I didn't know if I would continue working once I did. I was a woman in a predominantly male industry. It was the 1980s and there weren't many female role models—and certainly none who were pregnant! Nobody talked about it. It wasn't like today, with all the benefits we now have, including flexible maternity leave.

Once we decided to have children, I realized I had a great career, and it made financial sense to continue working. It was challenging to balance the priorities of a demanding career and a young family—and my experience of motherhood was even more challenging because my three children were all born prematurely.

Five years after I first put on my blue blazer and went to work, I welcomed my firstborn, Danny, into the world. He was born on the Fourth of July, which happens to be my birthday as well. Danny arrived six weeks early and had complications that required him to stay in the neonatal intensive care unit for the first six weeks of his life. His lungs were not fully developed and would have collapsed on their own; he needed supplemental oxygen to breathe. A year later, a synthetic surfactant would be discovered that would enable many preemies like Danny to breathe on their own. But at the time, we had no choice but to leave him in the NICU.

I had a six-week maternity leave, which I used to visit Danny in the hospital every day. Once he came home, however, I had to go back to work. It was difficult. I wished my family lived closer, and I began to understand why my mom had wanted us to live nearby.

I found a retired grandmother who helped me care for Danny, as he was too fragile to be in daycare. He progressed very well, however, and soon became a lively baby. I continued my career while also fulfilling the responsibilities of motherhood.

Five years later, we received the amazing news that we were going to have twins! My then-husband and I had been trying for years to have another baby, and now we were going to have two! The sonogram showed a girl and a boy. I was overjoyed!

I had a very difficult pregnancy with the twins, and my doctor ordered me to spend the last six months of it on bed rest. Little did I know, I was not going to make it through all six months.

I began to live my life from my bed. For a type A personality, in the age before iPads and videoconferences, this was crazy-making. I tried inventing little projects for myself, and Danny would come home from school and show me his latest magic tricks—but I couldn't imagine how I was going to endure so many weeks in bed.

Then my worst nightmare happened. I woke up at two o'clock in the morning to sheer terror: I was bleeding profusely. My then-husband drove me to the hospital. What the doctors prescribed made my two weeks of bed rest seem easy: they wanted me to stay in the hospital bed in an "elevated position," with my head down and my feet up in the air. It was uncomfortable and frightening, but it did stop the bleeding.

One night, a fit of coughing left my bed covered in blood. I rang the bell for the nurse, and when she came into my room, she made the sign of the cross. "I'll get the doctor," she called as she ran out.

My doctor was a high-risk obstetrician, and in the early hours of the morning, he acted quickly to get me straight into surgery. "It's serious," he explained. "You could die. Your babies could die."

They wheeled me into the operating room.

My twins were born on December 8, the Feast of the Immaculate Conception, after only twenty-eight weeks. Brian was three pounds, two ounces, the tiniest baby I had ever seen—until I saw Katie. My little girl was only two pounds, eleven ounces. Both of them were in neonatal intensive care. I could barely see their skin because of all the tubes that were hooked up to them.

I was beside myself when I found out Katie had a hematoma—a solid swelling of clotted blood within the tissues—in her brain. But as the weeks passed, the hematoma went away, and we had hope that she would make a full recovery.

The hospital sent me home a few days later, but they kept my two babies. Brian and Katie would stay there for the next three months, hooked up to tubes and monitors. The twins were the lucky recipients of the surfactant that had been developed too late to help Danny, and because of this miraculous treatment, they were able to breathe. Since I had only eight weeks of maternity leave, I had to go back to work, but it was almost impossible to concentrate with my babies in the hospital. I visited them every day, talked to them, watched them breathe, and prayed.

They were both discharged on the same day, February 28, their original due date. Both wore heart monitors that would sometimes go off in the middle of the night, the loud bells jarring us awake. I don't think any of us got a good night's sleep for that first year of their lives.

Miraculously, they survived, and grew strong and healthy. God had given me two terrifying pregnancies and three wonderful children. Today, Katie and Brian are amazing young adults, living their lives aware of God's purpose for them.

Life can be humbling at times, and having had such a difficult time bringing my children into the world helped me put my life in perspective. We will all encounter hardships. I have learned to pause and give myself permission to grieve, to be patient, and most importantly, to know that God has a plan. No matter how hard I try to control or change things, He will get me through.

These experiences also helped me put my career into perspective. My work was important, but it wasn't nearly as important as my family. My children have always challenged me, humbled me, and provided joys beyond anything a job could offer. They've also grown up knowing the challenges I faced early in life, and how hard it was for my parents to come to this country and leave their homeland behind.

Katie and Brian inspire me to be the best person I can be, taking a few steps forward and pausing in between in order to focus on what is important. We coach each other and respect our weaknesses while we work on the best version of ourselves. I am so proud of the adults that they have become.

CHAPTER 6

An Unexpected Twist

One day I received a phone call that would change my life's path again. The call was from a former colleague who was now the president of a giant Texas-based tech firm.

"I want you to come join us," he told me. "I promise you won't regret it."

He was right.

After I had been in my job for a year, there was a shake-up and the founder of the company, who had just lost the presidential election, came back to be the CEO. His assistant called me one day to ask if I knew anyone who spoke Spanish.

As far as I knew, nobody there knew that I was Cuban or that I spoke Spanish. I was still living in two worlds. I did not feel I had to tell people I was Cuban. I wanted to build my career outside of my identity as a Cuban. I felt burdened to have to explain the whole story of how we came to this country and why I was different from my colleagues. At that time, I didn't know of any coworkers who were Hispanic.

"Yes," I said. "I grew up speaking Spanish. Actually, Spanish is my first language."

"Great. Can you come up to the CEO's office immediately? It's a bit of a humanitarian situation."

"I'll be right up," I said.

When I got to the office, I saw a few men huddled around a speakerphone. At the head of the table sat our CEO, who looked relieved when he saw me.

"Marie is here!"

They offered me a seat and pushed the speaker closer to me. One of the men sitting near me whispered in my ear, "It's a kidnapping situation."

The man on the other end of the phone was in dire straits. Six years earlier, his son had been kidnapped, and he had since exhausted all his money on negotiating with the kidnapper and consulting with his attorneys. He had used every resource to try to get his son back. Now he was at wit's end, running out of money and running out of options.

"I am wondering if you might be able to help me," the man said.

The man next to me whispered again, "This happens more often than you might expect. People are always calling us, asking for humanitarian help."

As surprised as I was to discover this, I was even more stunned to learn that the company sometimes said yes to their requests. The CEO was a visionary who had made himself into a billionaire, and then into a household name.

"I'm not sure how we can help you," our CEO told the man. "But we're happy to try. Marie, can you go down to Costa Rica for a few days to see what you can sort out?"

That is how I wound up taking a private jet to Costa Rica so that I could begin negotiating for the release of a kidnap victim.

I flew out the next morning with a small, hastily packed suitcase. I wasn't really sure what I would be doing once I got to Costa Rica, and I didn't know how long it would take, so I had no idea what to pack.

Four hours later, the jet touched down in Costa Rica's capital of San José. And then I sat on the tarmac for another four hours.

"What is going on?" I asked.

The pilot pointed out the window.

"That is going on."

Next to our plane, I saw a swarm of Costa Rican police and US Secret Service and then, farther up the runway, Air Force One. The president of the United States had arrived in Costa Rica at the exact same time we had. As luck would have it, there was a trade and immigration summit in San José that week, and the heads of state from North and Central America were converging at the airport. There was nothing to do but wait until security cleared us to leave.

When I finally got out of the airport, I sat down with the man who had called our office. The kidnapping situation was even more complicated than we'd initially understood. The boy had been kidnapped by his own step-grandfather. Of course, the step-grandfather had his own side of the story, and because he was a relative, he claimed to have some legal rights to the boy. While the two parties argued, the step-grandfather kept the boy locked away in a compound outside the city.

The police couldn't determine whether the law considered the man's act a "kidnapping," so they refused to take action. Until we could prove to them that the father really did have legal rights to the boy, they would not intervene.

Apparently, this was not going to be an easy fix. I reported the news back to my boss.

"How would you feel about staying down there a while to sort this out?" he asked me. "Would you do that?"

I had three children of my own back in Texas, two thousand miles away. It was a difficult decision. After talking to my then-husband and my parents, and praying about it, I decided this was something I was called to do.

"Yes, sir," I told him. "I'll stay."

In the grand scheme of project management, this was a strange and interesting project, for sure. I learned more about the details of this family, and I learned some aspects of Costa Rican law. I met with lawyers and police, and I even worked with a Costa Rican Supreme Court justice. I traveled all over Costa Rica, meeting people in various cities to discuss the case and the various laws involved.

But everything took longer than expected. I would file a petition that I was sure would resolve the issue, but then the court would lose my paperwork. Or my filing would get overturned on some unforeseen technicality. Before I knew it, a full month had gone by.

"Mommy, when are you coming home?" my children asked me over the long-distance phone line. Danny was eleven and the twins were six.

"Soon," I told them, though I didn't know how soon. My boss flew my family to Costa Rica to visit me on several occasions, but it was still hard to sacrifice spending my days with them.

At the same time, a strange thing was happening to me. This was the first time I had lived, as an adult, in a country where Spanish was the native language and Hispanic culture was everywhere. I was eating foods that reminded me of the Cuban food my parents had cooked when I was a girl. The people here wore clothing that reminded me of what my grandmother wore.

Is this what it would have been like, I wondered, *to grow up in Cuba?*

I had spent all my childhood trying to assimilate and erase my Hispanic roots. And now here I was, living in a Hispanic country—and I loved it! I felt so much kinship. Though I had never been there before, Costa Rica felt like *home* in a way that New Orleans and Dallas never had.

Another month went by. We did more research on child custody law than I'd ever thought possible, and finally, it started to pay off. We discovered the United Nations Convention on the Rights of the Child, an international treaty that governs kidnapped children. This kidnapping was a clear violation of that treaty, which meant we didn't have to go through the Costa Rican courts at all. The step-grandfather was breaking international law.

We filed an international complaint through the court. Once again, I was sure this would finally bring the case to a close. Soon, the boy would be reunited with his family and I would be reunited with mine.

But it didn't happen. The case was dismissed.

Another month slipped by.

I went to the media, had articles and editorials published in the newspapers, and made appearances on television and radio. Soon, many people in Costa Rica became aware of the story. People even recognized me on the street: "You're that American looking for the kidnapped boy!"

As the visit and case dragged on, and even though we hadn't yet found the boy, I was finally able to go home.

As my plane lifted me out of the San José airport, I took one more look at the Costa Rican coast. Then, once we were higher in the sky, I also saw the outline of Cuba.

Though I didn't know it yet, I was getting close to making a trip to the land of my birth.

The case continued, and after months of tireless work that involved many people besides me, we were finally able to make legal claims against the step-grandfather, the authorities intervened, and the boy was eventually returned to his father.

To my surprise, a few weeks after my return to the United States, I received a phone call. "This is the US Ambassador to Costa Rica. I wanted you to know that, thanks to the efforts of you and your team, the Costa Rican government has decided to start the process to ratify the United Nations Convention on the Rights of the Child. This will hopefully help many families in the future."

I can't describe how it felt to receive that call. In corporate America, my work had rarely touched people's real lives—at least, not in such a meaningful way. I realized that, although I had been working hard for many years, the work I'd done during a few months in Costa Rica had a humanitarian purpose that I will never forget.

If you want to be happy and fulfilled, it's not enough just to find work. Success in business has many dimensions. To be successful, you must find what is important to you—*meaningful* work—that also challenges you and brings you purpose.

My work in Costa Rica had allowed me to reconnect to my Latina heritage, paving the way for my eventual return to Cuba. But it had also taught me that I was capable of more. I'd answered a call to do something that was not part of my career plan, *and I had helped change other people's lives.*

Answering the call had brought me to Costa Rica, but while I was there, I'd answered another call too. This trip turned out to be the seed that would bring about my return to Cuba years later. It now seems that I was destined to live in Costa Rica for a while, to speak Spanish every day and eat food that reminded me of my Cuban heritage. As someone once said, "Coincidence is God's way of remaining anonymous."

CHAPTER 7

Little Pearls of Wisdom

My firstborn, Danny, was an amazing young man who gave so much joy to everyone who was fortunate to know him.

Many years ago, Danny's preschool teacher asked me to come in after school to talk about my son. "Sometimes, in the middle of class, Danny will wander over to the window and stand there, completely still, to watch the men mowing the lawn," she said. "I call him back, but he doesn't answer. He just stands there."

I did not understand what she was getting at. "I guess he just likes lawn mowers," I said. This was true. I remembered him pointing out to me how the color of cut grass was different than the color of longer grass, and how the path of the lawnmower left patterns in the lawn, like drawings. He noticed the most interesting things.

But the teacher continued, "He has trouble paying attention. You may want to take him to see someone for testing."

Soon afterward, Danny was diagnosed with ADHD and learning disabilities. Like any parent, I wanted nothing but the best for my son. I wanted his life to be smooth and easy and full of riches, and without too much pain. These diagnoses broke my heart because each one meant that Danny's life would be harder.

I enrolled him in a small private school where he could receive a lot of individualized attention, and once he was in this environment, he was able to thrive. Despite all the new labels and diagnoses, he was still the same curious, kind-hearted boy. His new teachers loved him for his gentleness; in fact, he was always the teacher's pet.

Now that he was getting the care he needed, he didn't have any trouble picking things up or processing the information he was taught. He learned reading and writing and math like the other children, and he moved up through the grades right on time.

"I hate when people get angry at me and there's no reason to get angry."

Danny was sitting in front of me with a bruised eye and a cut lip. By now, he was in middle school, and a group of bullies had singled him out and wouldn't leave him alone.

I knew Danny would never, ever pick a fight; he would much rather be at home playing video games than pushing and shoving on the playground. But today, the bullies had grabbed his schoolbag from him and dumped everything out onto the ground. They had kicked his books and laughed as his homework blew away in the wind, and then they'd knocked him down and hit him.

"I'm not going back," he announced. "That's the only possible solution. I won't ever go back to school."

I held him tight.

"But you have to go back," I said. "There will always be bullies in the world, and your staying home from school will not change that. Hiding from them will not make them go away. The only thing you can do is prove that you are better than they are. Ignore their taunts, keep doing your work, and always be the better man."

Even at his young age, he seemed to take in what I'd told him and consider it with great seriousness. Then he told me, "OK. I've decided I will go back. But I can't promise you I'll always be the better man."

By the time Danny got to high school, doctors had diagnosed him with Asperger's syndrome, a mild form of high-functioning autism. He was shy and unathletic, but for some reason, the football coach noticed him and took him under his wing. He asked Danny to become the football team manager.

They say mentors are among our most important relationships, and that was absolutely the case with my son. Danny got to know the team, and he traveled with them on weekends to their away games. He learned everything he could about football, and he grew to love it, cheering from the sidelines, supporting his team. The team members treated him kindly and respectfully, like one of their own.

Being a team manager changed his life. It gave him friends, but more than that, it gave him confidence. In this role, he was accepted for who he was.

During the last game of his senior year, Danny told the coach he wished he could have been a football player, and the coach told Danny to suit up and play. "You've always been a member of this team," the coach told him, "so get out there!" Danny had one play on the field, and it caused him much anxiety, but it was the highlight of his high school years. At the end of the game, the coach and the rest of the team awarded Danny the game ball in gratitude for his commitment, devotion, and friendship.

Later that year, Danny told me he wanted to go to his senior prom. He had already asked the daughter of a family friend, and she had said yes.

"Is that OK?" he asked.

"That's great!" I said. I'd had no idea my son wanted to go to prom.

I took him shopping to try on a tuxedo. When he came out of the dressing room, I didn't even recognize him. I was so used to seeing him in jeans or sweatpants or shorts. He took my breath away.

"What do you think?" he asked.

What I thought was that Danny had grown into a handsome young man. I hugged him right there in the store and probably embarrassed him, but I couldn't help myself.

The night of the prom, I hired a driver and snapped pictures of him as he got into the car and left to pick up his date. I felt so good and so fortunate.

But just a couple hours later, I was washing dishes in the kitchen when Danny walked through the door.

"What's wrong?" I asked.

"Nothing's wrong. I just had the best night of my life."

"But why are you back home so early?"

He shrugged.

"We had a great dinner—I ate until I was totally full—and then we danced one dance, and I decided I was ready to come home."

"Aren't you supposed to stay until the end?"

"Mom," he explained, "we should do things because we want to, not because we're supposed to."

Then he changed back into his jeans and spent the rest of the night playing video games.

⁊

Danny had above-average grades and finished his senior year graduating sixth in his class. When the time came to pick a college, Danny's guidance counselors recommended we consider sending him to a school an hour north of Dallas—just far enough away for Danny to try living on his own, but close enough that we would still be able to see each other regularly.

I was not convinced the school, which was known mainly for its pre-med and pre-law programs, was a good match for my son. The curriculum was structured and rigorous. I worried it might put too much pressure on him and fail to give him the flexibility that had allowed him to thrive.

But the counselors thought this college would stimulate Danny and help him improve his self-discipline. They persuaded me that this was the best next step for his educational needs.

We drove Danny to his dorm, helped him unpack, and said our goodbyes. It was a difficult moment. I knew college would open opportunities for my son, but it would also put him through new challenges. Why couldn't there be a way to help our children grow but also spare them life's hard lessons? Of course, there isn't. But knowing Danny, I worried. Did he have the emotional skills to navigate this new chapter in his life?

At first, he settled in. During his first semester, he worked for the school newspaper as a sports writer. But he struggled with classes, and the worse that things got, the more panicked he became. He felt himself falling further and further behind. By the end of that first semester, his grades were poor and his self-confidence was in tatters.

Within days, the school called to let us know Danny had experienced some sort of breakdown and had been checked into a psychiatric hospital.

He had a new diagnosis, and it was a different type of mental disorder than we had thought he had.

Nothing can prepare you for learning that your child faces such a difficult and unpredictable daily battle. As a mother, you have so much hope for your children. You wish for them to be successful and have a wonderful life. And then one diagnosis changes everything.

So, you do all that you can do to hang on to hope. The grief is intense and the unfairness is hard to cope with. You push through your emotions and know in your heart that God does not give disabled children to everyone. He has called you for a greater purpose: to serve Him through the unconditional love of a special child, one who wants to contribute to the world in a way only he or she understands.

The adversity my son has survived in his first three decades is beyond what most adults have to endure in a lifetime. It is not fair, and sometimes I let myself get overwhelmed by it. Then my boy, my sweet gentle boy, will remind me: "We can only work with what we've got. But with what we've got, we'll keep working as hard as we can."

Danny worked hard, and finally, after eleven years, he graduated from college. He was featured on a local TV station as a "Texan with Character" for his perseverance in finishing his two-year college degree.

We were all very proud of him, and I decided to celebrate with a graduation party at home. All of Danny's favorite people attended, including his high school coach, who had always believed in him, and his best friend, Steve, who still takes time out of his day to call Danny and treat him to lunch.

My closest girlfriends, including my dear friend Sharon, were also there. These women knew that only God could intervene in Danny's life. We established a Bible study group because of Danny—one that we still attend to this day, to pray for one another, for our children, and for our purpose in life.

When Danny walked down the red carpet to the podium to receive his certificate, he was so happy. I could tell it was one of the proudest moments of his life. There were many touching speeches and many tears. My brother Raul wrote a beautiful letter, which he read aloud at the ceremony.

"I can assure you, Danny," Raul said, "that I don't have much in the way of great wisdom to give you. Instead, I want to share with you three things that *you* have taught *me*.

"First: **Live in the moment and embrace the things that we take most for granted with childlike eyes**, and even small annoyances will become magical moments. You've taught me to embrace the unexpected—yet amazing—things around us that we take for granted or look upon as daily annoyances. These are the moments that make life worth living.

"Second: **If you have the will, there is a way.** I look around this room and am sure there are many of us here who have multiple college degrees. Getting a college degree for us is the obvious step in obtaining a happy and productive life. Many of us never give it a second thought. Yet what you have done is so much more than just earning a college degree. What you have overcome makes all of our degrees put together seem so less important in comparison. You made a choice to persevere despite all the reasons not to, and by sheer will alone, you received your college degree. You taught me, Danny, that the power of the human will is truly limitless. If you have the will, there is a way.

"Third: **Believe in God, and everything else will fall into place.** The fact is, you are not alone, Danny, and you never have been. Your *will* will take you far, but your faith in God will help you climb mountains. You have lived through moments in your personal life that I could not imagine. You have so much to teach me in the way of faith in God that these few words can never begin to describe. You have taught me that God has a bigger plan for us than we do ourselves. Believe in God and everything will fall in place."

There wasn't a dry eye in the house when Raul was finished. I was amazed and humbled that my son had taught *grown men* so many things.

Danny is a gift to all of us. He left us too soon and I know that God needed him. We lost Danny on October 17, 2017, after he died of a pulmonary embolism during a routine hospital stay.

Danny left a legacy that has touched and impacted so many lives and continues to do so, especially at his former school, where the Danny Cummiskey Servant Leadership Scholarship is coveted by the middle school kids.

So many times we thought we were going to guide him with our wisdom, only to discover that he already has more wisdom than the rest of us combined.

CHAPTER 8

Reconnecting

From the moment my parents left their native Cuba and fled with me to the United States, they never stopped dreaming about the day they would be able to return home. Cuba kept tugging at them, calling them back. It was never far from their minds or hearts.

We have family who still live there. The sadness my mother and aunts and uncles experience when we get the news that a family member has passed on is immense. They can't help feeling that, even after fifty years, there might have been a chance we could have seen them again.

But we also always understood that we would never be able to go home to Cuba while Fidel Castro lived. Though the Castro regime has somewhat softened restrictions on travel visas over the years since my parents moved to the United States, it is still a communist dictatorship. Castro had a long memory for the people he considered traitors, and although he is now gone, today's government still has an army of bureaucrats whose sole job is to track Cuban defectors and make their lives difficult if they return to the island.

Even though my parents continued to eat and drink and dress and think as if they were Cubans, they also gradually came to understand that they would never go back—that the only Cuba they would ever see was the one that lived so vividly in their memories, in whatever communication came to them in letters, and in family visits. They did not like this fact, and they spent most of their waking lives resisting it. But slowly, reluctantly, they came to accept that it was the truth.

The part of them that dreamed of returning to their homeland receded. In old age, they finally gave up on the idea of going back, although their conversations were as though they had only arrived in America yesterday.

And then something happened.

My two brothers had already visited Cuba. Juan Carlos went first, in 1995, and came back with countless stories about everyone he had met on the island, including my father's brothers and sisters and their children and children's children. He told us how everyone was and how everyone lived. My father grilled him with endless questions. Every time Juan Carlos answered, it just reminded my father of more things he wanted to ask.

Juan Carlos also told me he had met my godmother, Cristina.

"She wants to know when you are going to visit, Marie."

"I can't go back without Mamí and Papi," I sighed. "I promised them."

But Juan Carlos had put the idea into my head, and it stayed there, tempting me, drawing me. *When was I going to visit Cuba?*

Three years later, Raul took his own trip, and he recounted his visit in a long, lovingly written letter to Juan Carlos and me. That letter left me feeling almost as if I had been there in Cuba alongside him . . . but also made me feel like I had missed out on something extraordinary and fundamental. His letter filled me with longing for something I was sure I would never see. As I finished reading the letter, I cried into a box of Kleenex. *This is as close as I will ever get to Cuba,* I thought after I'd read it.

I had promised my parents that I would not return to Cuba without them, and I took that promise seriously. But whenever I broached the idea of taking them with me for a visit, my father shut it down immediately. "It is not safe for us," he always said. "Not while Castro lives."

I never wanted to push the issue. My parents already felt enough stress about being away from Cuba without me pressuring them to risk a trip that might truly prove to be dangerous.

So I stopped thinking about it. "It will be fine," I told myself, "if I never go back to Cuba."

Little did I know what was in store for me.

In 2012, a miraculous opportunity came our way. The following year would mark the four hundredth anniversary of the miraculous appearance of the *Virgin de la Caridad del Cobre,* the Virgin of Charity who is the Patroness of Cuba. There was a rumor that the pope himself—at that time, Benedict XVI— would be traveling to Cuba to celebrate.

If the pope *did* go to Cuba, he would be accompanied by a contingent of other bishops, including my cousin Bishop Estevez, who was the bishop of St. Augustine. We'd never thought that we would get a chance to visit Cuba, but now circumstances were lining up so that we might get a chance to go after all, and on a religious pilgrimage that included the pope!

The odds of all this actually coming together were so remote that I did not take any of it very seriously. But in my heart, I felt a growing excitement. If everything worked out, I might finally get to visit my birthplace!

Then I got a call from Bishop Estevez.

"Marie," he said, "it's happening." But there was a catch. "If you want to go, you need to get all of your paperwork to the Archdiocese of Miami within five days."

The timing seemed next to impossible. My father was ill and had just moved into a nursing home. He was in no condition to travel. His failing health was putting stress on all of us, but on my mother most of all. Would she still want to go to Cuba in the midst of this? She always took a long time to deliberate before making important decisions, even under normal circumstances. And these were anything but normal circumstances.

She surprised us all when she told us, "Yes. I want to go."

She had concerns, of course. She had no intention of abandoning my father, who was adjusting to his new nursing home and even showed signs of improvement! "If his condition gets worse, then we will not go," she said. "But if this trip is something God intends for us to do, then we will do it."

My father's health was not the only obstacle we had to overcome. There was also an enormous bureaucracy that we had to navigate: we needed visas from Cuba and paperwork from the US, and we needed to find my mother's American passport . . . as well as her long-forgotten, fifty-year-old Cuban passport.

There were so many things that might go wrong. But we trusted that if God wanted us to go, everything would come together—and if not, then that was His plan, and we would accept that too.

Somehow, our paperwork came through. The matter was settled: although neither of us could quite believe it, my mother and I were going to Cuba!

The months leading up to the trip were difficult for my mother. It was almost as if the emotional toll of the anticipated trip was playing out physically, affecting her ability to move forward. She developed several illnesses and suffered several injuries, including a pinched nerve in her lower back that kept her from walking. I worried about how difficult the trip would be if she couldn't walk. Then my friend Tessie had a bright idea: we could bring a wheelchair.

Where there's a will, there's a way. We brought the wheelchair, and that trip was the only time my mother has ever used one in her life.

On the day of our departure, the airport was swarming with reporters who wanted to know why we were going back and what it felt like. Although our luggage had strict weight requirements, my mother had packed her bag with tiny gifts for each of her relatives. She had planned each gift carefully and thoughtfully, knowing that everyone in our family needed so much more than we would ever be able to carry. I don't know how she had any room left in her suitcase for her own things.

Aboard the plane, we sent our final farewell texts to our family, knowing that once we got to Cuba, there would be no cell phone reception and no Internet.

And then we took off.

A wave of excitement passed through the plane just a half hour later. I looked out the window and saw a bright-green island in the shape of an alligator: Cuba.

How could something that had loomed so large over my entire life have been this close all along? And how could something so close have felt so impossibly far away until today?

I touched my mother's shoulder and pointed out the window. When she saw it, she whispered, *"Mi Cuba,"* and her eyes overflowed with tears. Over and over she said it, her hand clasped over her heart as the tears streamed down her cheeks.

"*Mi Cuba. Mi Cuba. Mi corazón.*" *My Cuba. My heart.*

When we landed in Santiago de Cuba, passengers throughout the plane applauded and cried. I had arrived in Cuba—a sentence I did not think I would ever be able to say in my life.

We had come home.

Legend has it that four hundred years ago, three fishermen were struggling with the stormy waters of the Caribbean Sea. Fearing for their lives, they prayed to the Virgin Mary. The skies suddenly cleared, and when they did, the fishermen saw a wooden statue of the Virgin—completely dry and untouched by the storm. From that day on, the Virgin Mary was adopted as the protector of all Cubans.

The pope was in Cuba to celebrate the anniversary of this miracle, the appearance of *la Virgen de la Caridad del Cobre.* Pope Benedict would say a Mass in the city of Santiago, and then another, a week later, in the capital city of Havana, on the other side of the island.

Our bus was to take us directly to the Basilica of Our Lady of Charity of El Cobre to prepare for the pope's Mass. This drive was my first ground-level glimpse of Cuba since we'd left the country all those years ago.

Traveling through Cuba is like traveling back in time. You can see it immediately in the clothes people wear and in the cars they drive—it's like stepping onto the set of a movie from the 1950s.

Then you notice how few cars there actually are. There is almost no traffic in Cuba, a sobering reminder that very few people can afford to *own* a car.

There is also no advertising. Imagine driving through a major city without seeing any billboards! On our drive, the only signs we saw were handmade ones: *"¡Bienvenido a Cuba, Benedicto XVI Peregrino de la Caridad!" Welcome to Cuba, Pope Benedict, Pilgrim of Charity!* We also saw a few signs that were *not* handmade— official signage proclaiming, "Fifty Years of Socialism, Fifty Years of the Revolution."

We arrived at the stage where the pope would be saying Mass, and from where I sat, I could see people assembled for miles and miles. The pope spoke to the Cuban people with such kindness and compassion. And for the first time in my life, I felt myself to be one of them. When the sun dipped below the hills, it was the most beautiful sunset I have ever witnessed in my life.

That night, we were flown to Havana. We had one week left to spend in Cuba, and time has never seemed so precious to me. I had just one week to catch up on fifty years of absence from my extended family and my original home.

My first humbling moment was when we woke up, on our first day in Cuba, and went to a wonderful brunch in the hotel's restaurant. Two members of our family were going to meet us for brunch at the hotel—but they were not allowed to park in the hotel parking lot, and they were not allowed to eat in the hotel. The hotel was only for tourists, we were told. I could not believe it.

As we drove through the streets that day, my mother spoke in a low voice about the buildings we passed, and how she remembered them. Most were in a state of terrible ruin after many years of neglect. Havana looked like a city that had been hit by an earthquake or a bomb. I had a sense that the buildings themselves were grieving, crying to be returned to a sense of wholeness, to be reunited with the families who had once lived there and were now gone.

My mother sat up in her seat.

"Turn here!" she ordered my cousin, who was driving. She then commanded him to park and jumped out of the car.

"Wait!" I called after her. "Don't you want your wheelchair?"

"I don't need a wheelchair," she called back. "My legs recognize where I am."

The building had once been my mother's school. She walked through what must have once been a beautiful courtyard and turned a corner. I followed her into a small chapel with a Virgin Mary statue at the altar. There, she fell to her knees, and I knelt beside her.

"Thank you," she whispered, "for guiding our family through the rough waters and helping us to find a new life."

She turned her face toward me. "Thank you for supporting my sons and my daughter so that they could give guidance to their children, and for blessing our lives." She touched the floor in front of her. "This is where my faith started . . . here. And you have given me a path back to you so I can give thanks."

The next days were almost overwhelming. I met my father's brother Tío Cosme, now ninety-nine years old.

"My God!" he said. "You have brought me a miracle."

I met aunts and uncles and cousins, a family I barely knew but who knew and loved me—and were still a part of me, even across so much distance and time.

We visited the home where my mother had grown up, and where we had lived before we left Cuba. We walked through the dining room where my mother had eaten dinner every night with her family. She sank into the chair where her father had sat, and she cried.

We went back to the church where my parents had been married, the church in which I had been baptized. I experienced an incredible feeling of oneness, knowing that our family was reunited. I was overwhelmed with gratitude that God had given me the blessing of bringing my mother back to Cuba.

During that trip, something changed in me. It would not be quite right to say I discovered anything in Cuba, because what I discovered had been there all along: a sense of connection. I realized that, in my bones and in my blood, I am Cuban.

The pope's Mass in Havana was another celebration of *la Virgen de la Caridad del Cobre.* He spoke about the profound sense of peace in the Cuban people and said that, despite all the years of pain, the Virgin had always been and always would be by our side.

"*La Virgen nos une,*" he said, using a phrase that all Cubans know well: *the Virgin unites us.* I thought of my family, separated all these years by politics and tragedy, and I knew it to be true. *La Virgin nos une.*

My cousin Marty and I were asked by the priests to distribute rosaries to the people who were standing outside waiting for the mass. Hundreds of people opened their hands, and we handed out the rosaries . . . not realizing we were being captured on Cuban television. On the day we left, airport employees remembered us from that TV appearance and asked for a rosary.

Saying goodbye was terribly painful. There was no meaningful way to express what we *wanted* to say: "See you soon." Instead, we said, "May God continue to bless you and take care of all your needs."

My aunt handed me a box she had been keeping for fifty years. It held a charm bracelet my father had given to my mother, which my mother had left behind rather than risk losing it to the greedy guards at the airport. It also held my silver baby cup, now tarnished and dented, and my "baby book," which included a lock of my baby hair tucked into a little envelope.

"Tere," she said, "I have been caring for these for fifty years, hoping beyond hope I would be able to give them to you."

My tears would not stop. It felt as if I had been holding on to my emotions for my entire life, and now they were pouring out of me all at once.

Then we flew home.

It has now been more than ten years since our trip to Cuba. My mom is ninety-five years old. When I look at her today, I think of what a blessing it was that I was given the opportunity to take my mother back to the land in which she was born. I can see she would not be healthy enough to make that trip again now.

Time is precious. Don't waste it. A door is sometimes only opened once, and you get one chance to walk through it. To have taken my mom back to Cuba—to experience something that remarkable—was a gift only God could have made possible. Oh, what miracles we experience in this human life!

How I treasure the gift of finding myself. That little girl who went through so much pain and wanted to forget she was Cuban now stands as a grown woman. I am healing from that pain, knowing God led me to this miracle of going home with my mother. My heart is full of love and gratitude, and memories I will cherish for the rest of my life.

CHAPTER 9

Life Is Made for Dancing

When we are young, we think our parents will live forever. I think back to my father, in his fedora hat and his Guayabera shirt, and how he was ever the Cuban gentleman. Whether strolling on the beach in Miami, canoodling with my mother on a park bench, or posing for a photo, he exuded the sort of joy that said, "Come! Let's celebrate!" And celebrate he did.

But, of course, our parents won't live forever, and coming to terms with that fact is a terrible, inevitable part of adulthood.

A few months after my father's eighty-ninth birthday, he was diagnosed with Alzheimer's, and his illness came with a condition I had never heard of, called "sundowning." His confusion and restlessness got worse every night, after the sun went down, and then better with the light of day. As a result of this condition, he had a terrible time sleeping through the night. When dawn came, his symptoms would ease up and he would be calmer. Soon, he gave up trying to sleep at night. His nights became days and his days became nights.

Before his diagnosis, we had celebrated his eighty-ninth birthday with a big party full of his friends. My dad loved parties. "Life is a party," he would say, "and it is made for dancing!" He was nearly nine decades old, but that's what he did: he danced into the night, full of life, surrounded by friends. He didn't even

91

care what food we served, as long as we had good music so he and my friends could dance.

He was invincible.

I never imagined, as I watched him dance, that a year and a half later, he would be in a hospital with a failing heart. I thought my father would live to be a hundred. Actually, some part of me thought he would live forever.

But after his birthday party, his Alzheimer's progressed. Then, when he was ninety, his congestive heart disease got suddenly worse, and he was rushed to the emergency room with fluid in his lungs. The hospital kept him from dying that night, but we knew he would need care for the rest of his life. We had to move him into a nursing home.

I visited him at his new home every month. I met his new friends, who sometimes played dominoes with him. They laughed together and watched baseball games and napped. No matter what he was doing when I came to see him, my appearance would make him smile. He enjoyed his family visits more than he enjoyed anything else.

"How are you, Papi?" I would ask. I wanted to know about the food at the home, how they were treating him, and his health, but he would wave his hand to dismiss my questions.

"How are *you*?" he would ask back.

He always wanted to hear about whatever was happening in my life instead of talking about what was happening in his. It made him happy when I would tell him about his daughter and his grandchildren.

I visited him again the following month, and again just before a planned trip to Europe. My daughter had spent her last semester studying abroad, and we were going to tour the continent together. I wanted to pay my dad a visit before I left.

This time, Dad wasn't playing dominoes or laughing with his friends. I found him near the nursing home's entrance, sitting in his wheelchair, wearing his beloved baseball cap and one of his favorite blue shirts. He looked happy to see me, as always. But this time, he also looked tired.

"How are you?" I asked.

Instead of answering, he reached out to touch my face.

"I want you to know that I adore you," he said simply.

"Oh, Papi. *Yo te adoro mucho tambié*n." *I adore you so much too.* We both knew he did not have much time left.

I visited with him and then said goodbye. I knew, as I left, that I might not see him again.

I cried at the airport. I called my mother, wondering whether I should take my trip or whether it would be better to stay here with my dad. But she encouraged me to go.

"Marie, he would want you to be with Katie, having adventures, seeing the beauty life has to offer," she said. "He would want you to continue with your life."

I flew to Europe and met my daughter in Barcelona. Then we traveled through France and on to Portugal, where my brother Juan Carlos joined us. We visited the Sanctuary of Fátima in Portugal, where the Virgin Mary appeared to three shepherd children in 1917 and where pilgrims come to pray and give thanks. My daughter and I attended Mass in the beautiful basilica there, and in that holy place, I kept thinking of my father. I could not hold back my tears. Katie and I lit a candle for her *abuelo* and I told her that the Virgin Mary would be with him, when the time came, to carry him to Heaven.

That night, when we got back to our hotel in Lisbon, there were several messages from my brother Raul asking me to call him back. I did not want to hear what he was going to tell me, but reluctantly, I dialed his number.

"Marie," he said. "Dad died."

My heart broke into a million pieces. I had already known what my brother was going to say, yet nothing could have prepared me for the intense feeling of loss that overcame me. The man I had known and loved for every minute of my life, the man who had watched over me and believed in me, even when I did not believe in myself, was gone.

What could possibly have prepared me for that?

I called my mother. I could not even speak through my tears, and neither could she. Even if I could have spoken, I did not really know what to say. There was nothing to say. I just wanted to hug her and hold her.

We immediately began to make plans to fly back to the United States. Our family held an open-casket memorial service in Saint Petersburg, and there I was able to say my final goodbyes to my father. Mostly, I wanted to thank him for his countless gifts to me.

I knelt beside his open casket and spoke to him. It was like so many other conversations we'd had. One of my favorite things to do was to walk the beach with my dad, telling him about the events in my life and asking for his advice. I wanted one more walk on the sand, one more time to ask him what I should do about the problems I was facing at work and what I should do about my personal relationships. What I wouldn't have given for one more time to hug him on the beach and tell him how much I loved him.

"Papi, I want you to know what an inspiration you have been to me," I whispered. "When you were young, you made the hardest decision I can imagine. You left everything: your parents, your brothers, your sisters, your career, your home, your whole past, so we could be free and safe, so we could live in a country with freedoms we didn't have in Cuba. You came to the United States with nothing except us, your family.

"And after giving up so much, you could have chosen to live the rest of your life with regret and anger. But instead, you chose to live your life full of joy. Even in the midst of terrible sadness and unfairness, you always believed life is beautiful—the sunsets, the birds, the flowers, the relationships we make, and the moments we create with one another. Everywhere you looked, you saw the positive. You saw every life turn as a new opportunity.

"'Life is a party,' you said, 'and it is made for dancing.'

"Your positive energy gave me the courage I need to live my life. Thanks to you, I have the courage to try new things, and I have the faith that, no matter what I am doing, God will help me find the best path. Most important of all, you taught me that walking away from a bad situation sometimes requires even more strength than staying in one. Over and over, you have given me the courage and the integrity to walk away and start again. Thank you for everything.

"Goodbye, Papi."

When they took away his coffin, I had a feeling of wanting to ride away on it and disappear with him. Disappearing seemed better than trying to live without him.

But instead, using the strength he had taught me, I walked out of the church and found a way to start again.

We had one final funeral service in New Orleans, at the church my parents attended, and the one I went to as a young girl. Many of my father's friends came to pay their respects that day. He had touched many lives.

Perhaps best of all, we got a visit from my father's godson in Cuba, Alberto. My father had spent his life sending money to

Alberto, trying to help him, striving to stay connected to him and his family. Alberto had always dreamed of traveling to the United States so he could meet my father in person and thank him for so many years of love and support. The two of them never met face to face.

When Alberto heard about my father's passing, he was devastated. He said he hoped that he could attend the funeral, as was my father's wish. At the time, travel between Cuba and the United States was almost impossible, and we were told that making such a trip on short notice, for a specific date, was unthinkable.

But God had big plans. I had heard that the State Department occasionally makes special provisions when there is a death in the family, so I called everyone I could think of until I found a friend who had a friend who had a little clout with the consulate in Havana. Miraculously, we were able to get a visa.

My father was gone, but the perseverance I'd inherited from him had paid off.

At my father's funeral, Alberto met our family for the first time. He told us about the many kind things my dad had done for him over the years. In the days that followed, Alberto walked around the city wide-eyed. He went to his first American Major League Baseball game, shopped in his first Walmart, and wore his first wristwatch. I knew my father must have been smiling from Heaven, watching his godson experience so many new things.

When he got on the plane, a flight attendant offered him a Coke. He couldn't believe it. He hadn't had a Coke since childhood. Most amazing of all, this one was free. My cousin was stunned again when he walked into the New Orleans airport gift shop. You'd have thought he'd walked into the House of Bijan on Rodeo Drive. The trinkets, the toys, the mementos—he'd never seen anything like this before. Could such a store really cater to ordinary passengers?

He experienced yet more culture shock when we took him to a Kennedy Museum. We were surprised that he knew everything about JFK because, sadly, his country was still living in the early 1960s. Tragically, the current Cuba regime continues to restrict Cubans from their basic human needs. Cubans remain prisoners in their own country where legislation such as Cuba's Fishing Law (Law 129) puts a high penalty on fishing, which prohibits fishing and makes it virtually impossible to feed your family. Who ever heard of an island where it is unlawful for its citizens to fish and eat the fish from the sea?

Before Alberto left for home, my mom asked him to try on some of my dad's clothes, to see if there was anything he wanted to bring back with him to Cuba. Everything fit perfectly including my dad's shoes, which were small for a man's size. Alberto flew back to Cuba dressed in the clothes of his godfather, who continued to look out for his godson from Heaven

That is all we can hope for, really: to do so much good in our lives that the good outlives us, that our legacy continues to do good after we are gone.

Years have passed since then, but I still feel my father is looking out for me. Even though he is no longer here, he guides me from above, loving me and giving me strength. He still reminds me that, though life has its cloudy times, eventually the sun shines and breaks the clouds' grip . . . and the rainbow shines through.

His kindness and wisdom will never leave me.

Sometimes, since his passing, I try to imagine who my father would have been had he not left Cuba in November 1961. In America, my dad was the most positive person I've ever known. His mantra was, "You don't go back, even to get reinforcements."

This was a Cuban saying that meant you keep moving forward, never backward. Dad never wavered from this belief, even though he was separated from his parents and siblings, and even though he wished he could go back to get them all out.

Instead of letting Castro and all of his life's pain and challenges beat him down, my dad remained a half-glass-full personality. He never exuded anything but positivity, love, and generosity. My father always told his children that God shows you the way. God opens doors you never knew even existed. And God performs miracles.

In some ways, in our hearts, our parents really do live forever.

Three Lessons by Which to Live Life

Life is not fair. We have all faced adversity in our lives, and we will all face more of it before our lives are over. Today I realize that my immigrant mentality has enabled me to face difficult situations throughout my life. I have learned to pick myself up, let God do the heavy lifting, and trust that there will be better days ahead. I am shaped by my parents' story of how they got to the other side of their loss and, despite constant emotional pain, were able to model joy and love in their everyday lives.

I, too, have faced unspeakable loss: the loss of my father in 2012 and, six years ago, the tragic loss of my precious Danny. Danny's death brought me to my knees. I struggled with life, questioning how God could have allowed this to happen and trying to figure out how I could start over. In my struggles I searched for understanding and for comfort. I questioned whether I should finish this book. In my pain and sorrow, I trusted God, reminding myself that we are not in control of our lives. My faith reminds me that God works all things for the good. We decide how we are going to live, counting our blessings every day, being present with our family and friends, and intentionally looking for joy every day, taking one day at a time.

The losses I've endured in my youth and my adult life have felt unbearable at times, and I would never have been able to bear up under them without the love, faith, and connection that my father and mother planted in my heart. Every sentence here, from beginning to end, is imbued with the love I first found in my childhood home.

I want to share with you some of the biggest lessons I've learned in my life. These are the truths I have come back to, time and again.

1. Trust That You Can Start Over

Sometimes our most painful experiences offer the greatest opportunities to start over and focus on what is important. In the midst of pain, you will also find the guiding light and hope that will pull you forward.

Life is a constant cycle of change, and it can be easy to get off track. But there are lessons to be learned every time change knocks at your door, forcing you to change your priorities and start over. Know that whether you seek change or change finds you, your ability to embrace adversity is a critical part of your ability to live your life to the fullest.

My "White Dress Day" prepared me for life's challenges, and with my father's support, I faced that painful day with courage. I did not know it at the time, but the courage I learned that day would serve me well later in life, enabling me to start over when pain became unbearable and only darkness surrounded me. I passed through the clouds and found a double rainbow.

I have also learned many lessons from each of my varied careers. My path was not straight, and I found myself playing many different roles. Each of these roles offered me challenges, and opportunities to work on new skills.

I hope my experiences can inspire confidence in your fresh starts. Some of my personal and professional beginnings weren't welcomed, but life's unpredictability has taught me that growth often follows. Each experience equips you for the journey ahead, helping you navigate the twists and turns with resilience and determination.

A friend once told me something that has always stayed with me: "You spend your life chasing success, but then, once you get it, you need to stop chasing success and start chasing significance."

2. Embrace Your Authentic Self

One of the most important lessons I've learned is: "To thine own self be true." Embrace your authentic self by becoming aware of yourself and connecting to the innermost parts of your being.

This will mean something different to everyone, but for me, it means being the person God intended me to be. Sometimes we have to go through hard, humbling experiences to find out who we really are. The adversity we endure in life helps transform our character and brings out our true self. This connection with your soul is the only real connection you need. Your mind will trick you into believing you need to be someone you are not, and your environment will give you a false sense of security. The only way to live an authentic life is to connect with your deepest needs, and those needs reside in your soul.

That "Latina spice" I pushed aside for so many years is my heritage. I had to find myself to find my purpose. I had to find myself before I found my one true love, the love that God had me wait for. My husband, Jim, is my rock. It is a blessing that you can start over and find love again, and I am blessed to begin a new life with him.

Don't settle for anything but your authentic self. Your life's purpose will not be revealed until you can live freely within yourself.

3. Live Your Legacy Now

Your legacy needs to be lived in the present. The decisions you make on a daily basis become your legacy. Your legacy is an active way of connecting to your passion and your purpose while you are living it, every day. Your legacy becomes meaningful when you know not just *what* you're doing, but also *why* you're doing it. Time is your most precious asset. Live your legacy by making thoughtful decisions in every aspect of your life. Connect deeply to your purpose; it is now or never.

My legacy is about opening doors for others, just as my father opened the door for his family to live in freedom. Opening doors for others can be as simple as listening to someone's request for help. I have been able to use my stories and my connections to help others, and hopefully to shine a light on their path.

I live with the deep sense that every obstacle in my path was put there by God so that I can be an example to others. I know that this is a great responsibility, and that I must work very hard on myself if I am to be of help to others. I search for the meaning of events in my life and see God shining His light and His grace. My legacy is unfolding every day, and the decisions I make are part of a bigger purpose for living.

Finally, there is the legacy of my family, and our beloved Cuba. It is hard to forgive and forget. Even today, my family still talks about Fidel Castro and what he did to our country. Phrases like "should have," "could have," and "if only" make up the fabric of our lives.

I grew up dealing with the unfairness of one man's negative impact on so many people. Castro left an indelible mark on me. And today, although I know that I am exactly where I am supposed to be, I also have a responsibility to the part of my family that still suffers from life in a communist country. The conditions of life in Cuba today are hard to believe, and many people find them impossible to understand.

Political unrest. A messy divorce. A tragic loss of a child. These are the kinds of events in our lives that we want to run from. Life can sometimes be too painful and terrifying even to talk about, but when we find the courage to face our truths, they become a part of us. These essential experiences transform us into the people we're meant to be. Every painful experience, every single time you've had to start over, brings you closer to becoming the person God intended you to be.

There are no coincidences. You are exactly where you're supposed to be. None of your pain is without meaning. None of your past is lost. The journey is ongoing, and every hardship you have faced makes you stronger and brings you one step closer to becoming the person you are meant to be. **Nada se borra; nada se acaba.** *Nothing is erased; nothing ever ends.*

Take heart and have courage. Never be afraid to live life in a new way. Starting over might be the best and bravest thing you ever do.

Acknowledgements

I want to thank my mother, Antinea Estevez Quintana, whose love, strength, and empowering faith in God have helped me through my life. My mom has been graced with a lifetime of spiritual guidance and protection, a testament to her unwavering devotion to her Catholic faith, with a special reverence for the Virgin Mary, the Mother of God. She is a role model of selfless, unconditional love for me and our family. She was my voice in this book when we left on the last commercial Delta flight from Cuba. It was painful for her to remember, and I am ever so thankful for her love and support.

I want to thank my two brothers, Raul and Juan Carlos. I could not have written this book without their support, their words, and their unconditional love for me. They are my biggest critics and my biggest fans. I cannot say enough about their talent—Raul as an architect and writer, and Juan Carlos as an artist and counselor. Most of all, it is their human spirit that encompasses all that is good, humble, giving, and loving in this world.

I want to thank my husband, Jim, who has shown me that love never fails. He has supported me, loved me unconditionally, and helped me to heal my authentic self. His strong hold on me through the valley of darkness has helped me once again to find the rainbows. I have found the one whom my soul loves.

I want to thank my children, Katie and Brian, two loving and faithful young adults who are living their lives courageously. I admire their strength, their faith, their perseverance, their integrity, and their love for family. They have inspired me to finish this book, and I am blessed to have them as my children.

There are so many other family and friends to thank—my Uncle Charles, who introduced me to my grandmother's poem and whose memory of the pain of separation from Cuba inspired me to write this book. I want to thank my cousins Marty and Bishop Felipe Estevez, who helped me to find the courage to return to Cuba on a religious pilgrimage.

I also want to thank the many friends who have supported me, loved me, and helped me to get this book completed. Tessie, my childhood friend who has been with me through every important moment of my life, is the definition of a true friend, a sister whom I still look to for support and comfort. Sharon and Nan, who are like sisters, always there to encourage, support, love, and to be faithful servants to God. They have helped me to pick myself up when I have fallen and have encouraged me continuously to complete this book. I want to thank Fawn for her unfailing friendship and constant encouragement to write and finish this book.

I want to thank my stepchildren, Alexandra and Diana, and Diana's husband, Sean. I want to thank all my cousins and girl-friends, angels who pick me up when I fall.

Finally, and most importantly, I give thanks to God.

"For I know the plans I have for you," declares the Lord, plans to prosper you and not to harm you, plans to give you a hope and a future."

~Jeremiah 29:11 NIV

References

Video "Ed Sullivan interviews Fidel Castro," July 11, 1959, The Ed Sullivan Show, https://www.youtube.com/watch?v=kjpnfDwWd7Y. Retrieved on March 7, 2023.

Cuba Center, July 29, 2021, "Examining the Castro Regime's Internal Blockade on Cubans: How the Dictatorship Restricts Fishermen from Fishing," https://www.cubacenter.org/archives/2021/7/29/cubabrief-examining-the-castro-regimes-internal-blockade-on-cubans-how-the- dictatorship-restricts-fishermen-from-fishing.

"I hope you live a life you're proud of, and if you're
not, I hope you have the courage to start over again."
— *F. Scott Fitzgerald*

About the Author

Marie Quintana is a nationally recognized business leader and inspirational speaker. With a distinguished 30-year career in Corporate America, she has held executive leadership roles with industry leaders and Fortune 500 companies, including Tenet Healthcare, PepsiCo, Perot Systems and IBM.

Marie's remarkable contributions have earned her numerous prestigious accolades. She was recognized as one of the Top 50 Hispanic Women in Business by *Hispanic Business Magazine* and acknowledged as one of the Top 50 Women in Grocery by *Progressive Grocer*. She has been honored as one of the Top 5 Latina Executives by *Latina Style Magazine*, and in 2022, received the esteemed Latino Leaders Maestro Award for Professional Achievement.

Marie is dedicated to nurturing the development of the next generation of women leaders and throughout her career, she has actively mentored numerous female leaders. She was a founding board member of the Network of Executive Women and one of the leaders who co-founded the PepsiCo Women of Color Alliance.

Marie served on the Board of Directors for Fetch, a prominent leading shopper app, and the Board of Directors of Catholic Charities of Dallas.

Marie resides in Dallas, where she enjoys the company of her family, a wide circle of friends, and her beloved dogs.

www.ingramcontent.com/pod-product-compliance
Lightning Source LLC
Chambersburg PA
CBHW040734120726
48010CB00016B/375/J